WORK OF R.E.
IN THE
EUROPEAN WAR, 1914–19

THE ORGANIZATION AND EXPANSION OF THE CORPS, 1914–18

The Naval & Military Press Ltd

Reproduced by kind permission of the Central Library,
Royal Military Academy, Sandhurst

Published by
The Naval & Military Press Ltd
Unit 10, Ridgewood Industrial Park,
Uckfield, East Sussex,
TN22 5QE England
Tel: +44 (0) 1825 749494
Fax: +44 (0) 1825 765701
www.naval-military-press.com
© The Naval & Military Press Ltd 2006

Originally published as the final volume in the series

THE WORK OF THE ROYAL ENGINEERS IN THE EUROPEAN WAR, 1914-1918
MISCELLANEOUS

This section has been extracted from that title and follows the pagination of the original work.

In reprinting in facsimile from the original, any imperfections are inevitably reproduced and the quality may fall short of modern type and cartographic standards.

CONTENTS.

CHAPTER I.

	PAGE.
Peace Organization—Expansion on and after Mobilization—Subsequent Increase of Divisional Engineer Units and Signal Units	5

CHAPTER II.

Bridging Units—Army Troops Companies—Advanced and Base Park Companies—Electrical and Mechanical Companies—Tunnelling Companies	11

CHAPTER III.

Searchlight Company—Special Brigade—Labour Battalions—Printing Company — Field Survey Units — Anti-Aircraft Organization	16

CHAPTER IV

Works Companies—Forestry Units—Army Tramway and Foreway Companies—Inundation Section—Camouflage Park—Meteorological Sections—Reinforcement Companies—Coast Defence Units—Engineer Services	22

CHAPTER V.

Transportation Units, etc.	30

CHAPTER VI.

Army Postal Service	38

CHAPTER VII.

Depôts and Reserve Formations	43

CHAPTER VIII.

Officers—Engineer Staffs with Formations of the Expeditionary Force	48

CHAPTER IX.

Administration	58

APPENDIX.

Tables showing Growth of the Corps	61

CHAPTER I.

PEACE ORGANIZATION — EXPANSION ON AND AFTER MOBILIZATION — SUBSEQUENT INCREASE OF DIVISIONAL ENGINEER UNITS AND SIGNAL UNITS.

PEACE ORGANIZATION.

IMMEDIATELY prior to the outbreak of the European War in August, 1914, the Royal Engineers consisted of the following units:—

	At home.	Abroad.	Total.
Field Squadron	1	—	1
Field Troop	1	—	1
Field Companies	13	2	15
Bridging Trains (*Cadres* only)	2	—	2
Signal Squadron	1	—	1
Signal Troops	5	—	5
Divisional Signal Companies	6	1	7
Cable and Airline Sections	2	—	2
G.P.O. Signal Company	1	—	1
Printing Company	1	—	1
Railway Companies	2	—	2
Works L. of C. Company	1	—	1
Fortress Companies (Coast Defences)	11	15	26
Coast Battalion Companies (Coast Defences)	2	—	2
Survey Companies	3	—	3
Depôt Companies	9	—	9
Training Depôt for Field Units	1	—	1
Railway Depôt	1	—	1
Special Reserve Units—			
Siege Companies	2	—	2
Railway Companies	3	—	3
Depôt Companies	2	—	2
Postal Section	1	—	1
Signal Section	1	—	1

There were also various establishments not recognized as units. These were *Battalion Headquarters* at Chatham, at Aldershot and for the Survey Companies, *Establishment for Engineer Services, School of Military Engineering, Depôt Office, School of Electric Lighting, School of Signalling, War Office, R.M.C., R.M.A. Staff College, N.C.O.s for duty in General Staff Offices,* and the *Indian Establishment,* including *H Company*. The total establishment of the Royal Engineers (excluding Special Reserve) was :—

        1,078 officers   9,171 other ranks.

The establishment of the Special Reserve was :—

        37 officers   1,200 other ranks.

In addition there were

	Officers.	Other ranks.
Signal and Motor Cyclist Sections, S.R....	3	468
Postal Section, S.R.	10	270
	13	738

The total establishment of Regulars and Special Reserve was

        1,128 officers   11,109 other ranks.

EXPANSION OF UNITS ON MOBILIZATION.

On mobilization the following Engineer and Signal Units required for the Expeditionary Force of six Divisions were provided from the above units, brought from peace to war establishments :—

Divisional Units—
    Field Companies, 6 × 2 12
    Divisional Signal Companies 6

Cavalry Divisional Units—
    Field Squadron 1
    Signal Squadron 1
    Signal Troops 4

Cavalry Brigade Troops (not allotted to Cavalry Division)—
    Field Troop 1
    Signal Troop 1

Army Troops, etc.—
    Works L. of C. Company 1
    Fortress L. of C. Companies 2
    L. of C. Signal Company 1
    Railway Companies 2
    Printing Company 1
    H.Q. of G.H.Q. Signal Company 1
    H.Q. of Army Signal Companies 2
    Airline Sections 5
    Cable Sections 10
    Wireless Section 1
    Railway Transport Establishment
    Survey Sections
    Postal Offices
    Various

The Cable and Airline Signal Sections and G.P.O. Signal Company were organized in peace with a view to considerable expansion in war, and from them, supplemented by personnel from the Army Reserve and the Signal Section Special Reserve, the following units were formed on mobilization :—

    1 H.Q. of a G.H.Q. Signal Company.
    2 H.Q. of Army Signal Companies.
    5 Airline Sections.
   10 Cable Sections.
    1 Wireless Section.
    1 L. of C. Signal Company.

Only a small cadre of ten N.C.O.s and men for each Bridging Train existed in peace, and these cadres had each to be expanded to an establishment of 302 N.C.O.s and men on mobilization.

Reinforcements for the R.E. units of the Expeditionary Force were in the first place found from the various depôts in England, as follows :—

For Field Companies—Mounted men from the Training Depôt, Aldershot ; dismounted men from the Reserve Battalion and Depôt Companies at Chatham.
For Signal Units, from Reserve Signal Company, Aldershot.
For Railway Units, from Railway Depôt, Longmoor.
For Postal Units, from Home Depôt, Postal Section.
Other Units, from Reserve Battalion and Depôt Companies, Chatham.

Expansion after Mobilization.

In August, 1914, very shortly after the outbreak of hostilities, orders were received to form the 7th Division. To provide the necessary Engineer and Signal Units, the 54th Field Company, the 55th Field Company, and the 7th Divisional Signal Company were selected. The 54th Field Company was at Chatham—the 55th Field Company and the 7th Divisional Signal Company were brought home from South Africa. In September, 1914, before the 7th Division was sent to the theatre of war, orders were received to form the 8th Division. For this Division the 15th Fortress Company was brought home from Gibraltar and converted into a Field Company, the 2nd Field Company was brought home from Egypt and the 8th Divisional Signal Company was raised as a new unit. Orders were also received in August, 1914, for the formation of

    2nd and 3rd Field Squadrons,
    2nd and 3rd Signal Squadrons.

The 2nd Field Squadron was formed with the 4th Field Troop as a nucleus. Surplus personnel of the 2nd Field Squadron, for which a modified establishment had been approved, served as a nucleus for the 3rd Field Squadron. The 2nd Signal Squadron was formed overseas and the 3rd in England. Two additional Signal Troops (6th and 7th) were formed from Cavalry units in the 6th and 7th Brigades in September, 1914.

ADDITIONAL FIELD COMPANY FOR EACH DIVISION.

In September, 1914, a recommendation was received from G.H.Q., France, that another Field Company should be added to each Division (making three per Division). The provision of three Field Companies per Division had been recommended by Lord Kitchener's Committee in 1912. On approval to the recommendation from France being given, arrangements were made to provide eight Field Companies from the Territorial Force to complete the first eight Divisions.

FORMATION OF R.E. UNITS FOR NEW ARMIES.

A short account has now been given as to how the Engineer and Signal Units for the first eight Divisions were provided. The decision to raise new Armies involved the raising of the necessary Engineer and Signal Units for them, and the requirements of war rendered necessary the formation of various kinds of special units. A short account of how these units were provided follows.

FIELD COMPANIES.

For four new Armies, each of six Divisions, steps were first taken to raise 48 Field Companies, *i.e.*, two per Division. Cadres for these Companies were formed at Chatham and sent to the Training Centres allotted to them. They were then completed to establishment by drafts from Chatham, as men became available.

In January, 1915, after the above 48 Companies had been formed, it was decided to add a third Field Company to each new Army Division. This was effected as follows: The twelve Field Companies of the 3rd Army were transferred to the 1st and 2nd Armies, thus raising the number of Companies in each of the two latter Armies to 18. The additional Companies for the 3rd Army and Companies for the 4th and subsequent Armies were then raised as new units. Eventually 93 new Field Companies were raised, of which 33 were raised by local bodies, municipalities of towns, etc.

When the Field Companies referred to above had been sent overseas, the Territorial Force was called on to provide Field Companies for additional Divisions as required, with the resultt hat in December,

1918, the total number of Field Companies serving overseas was as follows:—

	Regular.	T.F.	S.R.	Total.
France	93	64*	2	159
Egypt	3	9	–	12
Salonika	8	5	–	13
Italy	5	4	–	9
Mesopotamia	3	3	–	6
	112	85	2	199

The 93 Regular Field Companies in France included three Companies of the Royal Naval Division, the personnel of which was transferred to the R.E. from the Royal Marines.

In consequence of a hope expressed by the Government of India in June, 1918, that it would raise an additional half million combatants, approval was given to the formation of Sapper and Miner Units to replace the Field Companies—and also the Field Squadrons and Troops, and Army Troops Companies—in Egypt, Salonika and Mesopotamia. 190 British officers were to be sent to India for these Sapper and Miner Units. Owing to the cessation of hostilities in October and November, however, only a small portion of this reorganization actually took place.

FIELD SQUADRONS AND FIELD TROOPS.

Only one Field Squadron (1st) and one Field Troop (4th) existed on mobilization. The subsequent formation of 2nd and 3rd Field Squadrons is referred to above. The 6th, 7th, 8th and 9th Field Troops were subsequently formed in Egypt for service in Egypt and Salonika, and towards the end of 1915 the 4th and 5th Field Squadrons were formed in France, for duty with the 4th and 5th (Indian) Cavalry Divisions.

During the latter part of 1916 the two Field Troops which were at Salonika were sent to Egypt, and during 1917 an additional Field Troop, known as No. 10 Imperial Camel Brigade Field Troop, was formed in that country. There were then five Field Troops in Egypt—6th, 7th, 8th, 9th and 10th. During 1918 the 6th, 7th and 9th were converted into No. 6 Field Squadron, and the 8th and 10th into No. 7 Field Squadron.

* Six of the T.F. Companies in France were sent out in July, 1918, on a slightly reduced establishment for work on the L. of C. They did not accompany Divisions overseas.

Owing to the reduction of the number of Cavalry Divisions in France from five to three, the 4th and 5th Field Squadrons were broken up in April, 1918. The personnel of these units was mostly utilized as reinforcements for the 1st, 2nd and 3rd Field Squadrons, but a Field Troop was formed from it, and sent to India with a Cavalry Brigade.

The number of Field Squadrons and Field Troops serving overseas at the end of 1918 was

Field Squadrons—France	3
Egypt	2
Total	5
Field Troop—Mesopotamia	1

SIGNAL UNITS.

The growth and development of Signal Units to meet the requirements of modern warfare has been dealt with in the volume of this history relating to the Signal Service. The subject, therefore, is only briefly mentioned here.

The Regular Signal Units which existed at the outbreak of war have already been referred to—in addition to these there were 14 Divisional Signal Companies and five Army Troops Signal Companies of the Territorial Force. By the end of the war these units had increased to seven G.H.Q., 24 Corps, 64 Divisional, and five Cavalry Divisional Signal Companies, besides numerous units of other descriptions. The total establishment of the regular Signal Service for the original Expeditionary Force was 78 officers and 2,387 other ranks. In November, 1918, there were 2,116 officers and 56,792 other ranks of the Signal Service serving with the various Expeditionary Forces.

Chapter II.

BRIDGING UNITS, ARMY TROOPS COMPANIES, ADVANCED AND BASE PARK COMPANIES, ELECTRICAL AND MECHANICAL COMPANIES, TUNNELLING COMPANIES.

Bridging Units.

As before mentioned, only two Bridging Trains were formed for the original Expeditionary Force, but it was decided later that each of the New Armies was to include

>   1 Horsed Bridging Train,
>   1 Mechanical Transport Bridging Train.

These Trains were formed gradually, four Horsed Bridging Trains being formed first and subsequently Horsed and M.T. Trains in turn. The units were sent overseas as they were formed, and when the last of them embarked in October, 1916, the total number of Bridging Trains with the British Armies in France was twelve. The 9th and 11th (Horsed) Trains were, however, converted to M.T. before they proceeded to France.

The name of these units was changed from " Bridging Trains " to " Pontoon Parks." The Pontoon Parks (Horse Transport) were R.E. Units, and the Pontoon Parks (Mechanical Transport) were R.A.S.C. Units for purposes of administration. An establishment for a Bridging Park for a Cavalry Corps was approved in January, 1917. In February, 1918, a Pontoon Park was approved for Egypt and designated the 13th Pontoon Park, but the Field Company establishment was reduced in personnel and animals to an equivalent extent.

In September, 1918, it was decided that it was necessary to form special Bridging Units whose primary function would be the bridging of canals and rivers for the passage of tanks. At a conference held in that month it was decided to form three Battalions, and that they were to be R.E. Units. Christchurch was selected as the place for their formation, the 5th Reserve Battalion, R.E., hitherto stationed there, being abolished. The three Battalions and a Bridging Training Centre Headquarters were assembled at Christchurch early in November, 1918. All the senior officers and about half the junior officers were withdrawn from France, the remaining officers and all the N.C.O.s and men were found from reinforcements available at home. A few technical officers and N.C.O.s were transferred from the Tank Corps. Technical tank training was carried out at the Tank Corps Training Centre, Wool, to which batches of officers and other ranks were sent for courses. The Bridging training was carried out at Christchurch, entirely under R.E. arrangements. In December, 1918, in view of the Armistice the number of battalions was reduced to one.

ARMY TROOPS COMPANIES.

In July, 1915, the Field-Marshal Commanding-in-Chief recommended certain changes in the organization and establishment of Fortress Companies for duty on the L. of C. These proposals were approved, and, on the suggestion of the C.I.G.S., these units were renamed "Army Troops Companies." Steps were taken to bring all the Fortress Companies with the Expeditionary Forces up to the new establishment for an Army Troops Company. At that time there were in France four regular Fortress Companies (20th, 25th, 31st and 42nd) and ten Territorial Force Fortress Companies. The 20th and 42nd Companies went out with the original Expeditionary Force, but the 25th and 31st Companies had since been brought home from Hong Kong and Ceylon respectively, and converted into Fortress Companies for duty on the L. of C. A detachment of the 31st Company was left in Ceylon and subsequently became the 48th Fortress Company, R.E. Two Regular (14th and 37th) and two Territorial Force Companies were serving with the Mediterranean Expeditionary Force, the Regular Companies having been formed from the 14th Survey Company. In consequence of a decision that there should be one Army Troops Company for every Division of an Expeditionary Force, 41 Companies were formed in addition to the Companies mentioned above. They were formed in the same way as Field Companies were formed, 13 of the 41 being raised by local bodies. In December, 1916, authority was given for the formation of the 166th (Guernsey) Improvised Field Company, composed of men recruited in Guernsey and Alderney. In February, 1918, this unit was utilized to form the 245th (Guernsey) Army Troops Company, which embarked for France in April, 1918, and the 166th (Guernsey) Fortress Company, which remained in Guernsey.

As the number of divisions overseas increased, so did the number of Army Troops Companies, and, in addition to the Companies required on the scale of one per Division others were required on the L. of C. When all the Regular Army Troops Companies had been utilized, further Companies were formed from the 2nd Line Fortress Works Companies (T.F.), which were converted into Army Troops

Companies as required. In December, 1918, the number of Army Troops Companies serving in the various theatres of war was :—

	Regulars.	S.R.	T.F.	Total.
France	39	1	12	52
Egypt	3	–	4	7
Salonika	7	–	–	7
Italy	1	1	–	2
	50	2	16	68

The establishment of each Army Troops Company in France was reduced by eight other ranks in December, 1918 (*see* under Electrical and Mechanical Companies).

ADVANCED AND BASE PARK COMPANIES.

It was decided by the Army Council in February, 1915, that two Works Companies, R.E., were to be provided for each of the two Lines of Communication in France, so that four Works Companies were required. It was, however, subsequently decided that two of these Companies should be called " Advanced Park " and two " Base Park " Companies, as the term " Works Company " as applied to such units was confusing. One Company (the 29th Works Company) already existed. The 24th and 32nd (Fortress) Companies had already been brought home from Malta and Gibraltar, and were being converted at Chatham into Fortress Companies. They were sent to France for conversion into two Base Park Companies. To provide the fourth company, the 1st (Fortress) Company was brought home from Gibraltar, converted into an Advanced Park Company, and sent to France.

Developments in Egypt and subsequently at Salonika necessitated the formation of Advanced and Base Park Companies for those places. Two Advanced Park Companies were raised by the conversion of the 4th (Fortress) Company, R.E., and of half the 19th Survey Company. These units, which after conversion were known as the 4th and 46th Advanced Park Companies, were sent to Salonika and Egypt respectively. Both were raised on a modified establishment, but the 46th Company was subsequently raised to the same establishment as an Advanced Park Company in France. It finally became a Base Park Company.

The two Base Park Companies required were provided by the conversion of the 33rd (Fortress) Company and the 13th (Survey) Company. The 33rd and 13th (Base Park) Companies were raised on modified establishments, but were subsequently raised to the same establishment as the Base Park Companies in France. They were sent to Egypt and Salonika respectively. The 47th (Fortress) Company, which had been sent home from South Africa, on the reorganization of the South African Defences, was converted into a Base Park Company on a modified establishment and sent to Mesopotamia, on the application of the C.-in-C. in India for a Base Park Company for Mesopotamia.

In August, 1916, the establishments of Base Park Companies in France were increased, but not those of Companies in other theatres. In September, 1917, the 358th Special Base Park Company was formed in East Africa from details of the 47th Company in South Africa. Its final establishment was two officers and 34 other ranks. In November, 1917, the 389th Advanced Park Company was formed at Chatham for work on the L. of C. in Egypt. Its strength on formation was five officers and 106 other ranks, but all the above did not embark, as certain tradesmen were available for the Company in Egypt.

In January, 1917, the Field Marshal Commanding-in-Chief in France recommended that, as the existing Base Park Companies were incapable of handling the constantly increasing quantity of R.E. stores, which amounted to 200,000 tons per month,

(a) the 24th Advanced Park Company be converted to a Base Park Company;

(b) that four new special store sections should be formed and that two sections should form part of each Base Park Company. Hitherto there had been only one such section per company;

(c) The whole of the personnel of the Base Park Companies should be men without military training and above military age, but possessing the necessary trade qualifications;

(d) The officers commanding Base Park Companies should be Majors.

These proposals were approved in February, 1917. In September, 1918, the 29th Advanced Park Company in France was converted into a G.H.Q. Troops Company, to perform the work of an Army Troops Company in the G.H.Q. area, with a new establishment of five officers and 104 other ranks. Prior to this all work formerly carried out by Advanced Park Companies had been taken over by Base Park Companies.

ELECTRICAL AND MECHANICAL COMPANIES.

One of these units was formed for France in September, 1915, and one for Mesopotamia in September, 1916. The unit for France was formed from personnel of the Tyne and London Electrical Engineers (T.F.) and was therefore a T.F. Unit. The unit for Mesopotamia was composed of Regular personnel and was designated the 300th Electrical and Mechanical Company, R.E. In November, 1916, the

Field Marshal Commanding-in-Chief in France represented that the number of machinery plants was far greater than one company could deal with, and recommended the formation of five Electrical and Mechanical Companies—one for each Army. The establishment recommended was

    4 officers,   259 other ranks,

as against the existing establishment of

    4 officers,   123 other ranks.

In order to provide, in part, the personnel for these Companies, the Field Marshal Commanding-in-Chief suggested a reduction of eight other ranks in the establishment of an Army Troops Company and of 16 other ranks in that of a Siege Company, and the reduction of one Land Drainage Company. By this arrangement the total number of officers and other ranks to be found from England was reduced to

    12 officers,   531 other ranks.

These proposals were approved in December, 1916, and the numbers 350 to 354 were allotted to the five Electrical and Mechanical Companies. In January, 1917, two additional Companies were formed from low category men in France for employment on the L. of C., and the numbers 355 and 356 allotted to them.

TUNNELLING COMPANIES.

These units were formed in France, for mining operations in that country, from men employed in the mines of Great Britain. Their formation commenced early in 1915. Personnel for some companies was enlisted in England and sent overseas in weekly drafts—personnel for other Companies was transferred from infantry, etc., serving overseas. Twenty-five Companies were raised on an establishment of 14 officers and 307 other ranks. Early in 1916, as it had been found necessary to attach parties of infantry to increase the effective strength of Tunnelling Companies, the establishment of 20 Companies was raised to a strength of 18 officers and 530 other ranks, the remaining five "Lower" Establishment Companies remaining at the original strength. The Companies never actually reached the full strength of the Higher Establishment, as the Board of Trade and mine owners intimated that no more miners could be spared without seriously interfering with the mining industry in England.

Men rated as tunnellers at first received 6s. a day, and tunnellers' mates 1s. 2d. a day regimental and 1s. a day Engineer pay; but in 1917 these special rates were abolished, and men of Tunnelling Companies received ordinary R.E. rates of pay.

Further details of the establishments, organization and work of the units referred to in this chapter will be found in the subsequent sections of the volume, and also in other volumes of the series already published.

CHAPTER III.

SEARCHLIGHT COMPANY, SPECIAL BRIGADE, LABOUR BATTALIONS, PRINTING COMPANY, FIELD SURVEY UNITS, ANTI-AIRCRAFT ORGANIZATION.

SEARCHLIGHT COMPANY.

A Company, called the 50th Searchlight Company, was formed in England and proceeded overseas in April, 1916. Subsequently the establishment of each Field Company was increased by 13 other ranks to work the oxy-acetylene searchlights provided for those units. These searchlights were, however, found not to be as useful as was expected, and the Field Companies reverted to their original establishment.

An account of Anti-aircraft Searchlight organization is given in a later section of this volume.

SPECIAL BRIGADE.

In the summer of 1915 Special Companies for the use of gas were formed in France in the G.H.Q. area. The personnel was found from men with qualifications as chemists, specially enlisted at home or transferred from other arms. These companies were first employed at Loos in September, 1915. Owing to the difficulty in keeping them up to establishment, and as it was not considered that the whole of their personnel need be specially qualified, B1 men were transferred to them from Reserve Garrison Battalions.

The Special Brigade subsequently expanded to such an extent that Battalions were formed. In addition, there was a Special Brigade Depôt at Helfant and detachments at the Headquarters of each Army, Corps and Division. The companies were of three types, Cylinder, Mortar and Projector Companies. At the cessation of hostilities the Special Brigade in France consisted of

        Headquarters and Depôt,
        16 Cylinder Companies,
        1 Projector Company,
        4 Mortar Companies.

LABOUR BATTALIONS, R.E.

Owing to the increasing difficulty in finding sufficient personnel for roadmaking, etc., it was decided in June, 1915, to form Labour

Battalions from men of the navvy class for such work. The personnel were to be over military age, and to be enlisted at a special rate of pay—3s. per day. It was originally intended to form 16 Battalions, but only 11 were actually formed, for work in France. A battalion, designated the 18th, was raised in Ireland for work in Salonika, but owing to the difficulty of obtaining recruits it was sent overseas on a modified establishment.

It was subsequently decided that the 11 Labour Battalions in France should be replaced by Infantry Works personnel as casualties occurred. The Labour Battalions were finally transferred to the Labour Corps in the early part of 1917, and the Depôt which had been formed at Southampton to deal with personnel for them was abolished.

Land Drainage Companies.

Two Land Drainage Companies—the 196th and 197th—were formed for work in France, the personnel being drawn from the Fen district, and being paid 3s. a day.

The number of companies was reduced from two to one in December, 1916 (*see* under Electrical and Mechanical Companies).

Printing Company.

The Printing Company, which formed part of the original Expeditionary Force, had various sections added to it. In 1914 in France its establishment was one officer and 39 other ranks, and it consisted of a Headquarter and four Printing Sections.

The Army Printing Sections were transferred to Field Survey Companies on the formation of these latter units.

There were also three Printing Sections in Egypt, East Africa, and Salonika.

For further developments of the Printing Company in France, *see* under Field Survey Companies and Battalions.

Field Survey Companies and Battalions.

Three Survey Companies—the 13th, 14th and 19th—existed prior to mobilization, their personnel being employed under the Board of Agriculture and Fisheries. On mobilization the 13th and 14th Companies were split up into half-companies and allotted for employment in Coast Garrisons in England and Ireland. After mobilization, as the work in these garrisons was taken over by the Territorial Force, these units were utilized as follows :—

The 13th Company was converted into a Base Park Company for Egypt.

B

The 14th Company was converted into two Army Troops Companies—one of which was numbered the 37th—for employment in Egypt.

Half of the 19th Company was converted into the 46th Advanced Park Company for Egypt.

The other half of the 19th Survey Company was stationed at Southampton and acted as the Reserve Depôt Company for all the Field Survey Units overseas.

Topographical Sections.

Four of these Sections were formed in France after the outbreak of war—they were afterwards incorporated in the Field Survey Companies. In addition to these the 5th and 6th Topographical Sections formed parts of the forces in Egypt and East Africa respectively, and there was also a Section in Salonika.

Field Survey Companies.

Four of these companies were formed in France in March, 1916, and on the recommendation of G.H.Q., France, they were recognized as R.E. units in July, 1916. They were organized to combine various sections into one unit. A Field Survey Company comprised:

    Headquarters,
    Topographical Section,
    Map Section,
    Observation Section,
    Sound-Ranging Section,

such of the above sections as already existed in France being absorbed into Field Survey Companies.

Later, the Army Printing Sections were transferred from the Printing Company to the Field Survey Companies.

In February, 1917, an establishment for a Field Survey Company to absorb the Topographical Section, Maps and Survey Section and Printing Section at Salonika, was approved.

Sound-Ranging and Observation Section.

In order to locate the position of guns in action it was decided, early in 1915, to form " Ranging and Survey Sections." They were, however, subsequently replaced by Army Topographical Sections, which were finally incorporated in the Field Survey Companies.

As the value of these sections became more and more evident, more and more Sound-Ranging Sections and Observation Groups were formed. In November, 1918, there were 25 Sound-Ranging Sections and 24 Observation Groups in France, distributed among the

Field Survey Battalions. There were also Sound-Ranging Sections and Observation Groups in Italy, Egypt and Salonika.

In January, 1918, Sound-Ranging and Observation Sections were added to the establishment of the Field Survey Company at Salonika; these were formed in France. In May, 1918, the 26th Observation Group (two officers and 66 other ranks) was sent from Italy to Salonika. In January, 1918, on the recommendation of the G.O.C.-in-C., the Field Survey Unit with the Egyptian Expeditionary Force was reorganized.

This reorganization entailed the addition of 11 officers, 66 other ranks and 45 batmen, and provided for the absorption of the Meteorological Section into the establishment of the Survey Company, which became a Field Survey Company. In June, 1918, an Observation Group (No. 28) was sent to Egypt from France and was included in the establishment of the Field Survey Company.

On the dispatch of the British Force to Italy from France, it was accompanied by a portion of the 2nd Field Survey Company. This was subsequently formed into the 6th Field Survey Company in Italy.

The Field Survey Companies serving overseas in May, 1918, were as follows :—

- 1st, 3rd, 4th, 5th, and Depôt Companies ... ... France,
- 6th Field Survey Company ... ... Italy,
- 7th Field Survey Company ... ... Egypt,
- 8th Field Survey Company ... ... Salonika.

FIELD SURVEY BATTALIONS.

In order to regularize the establishment of skilled personnel attached to Field Survey Companies in France and to enable this personnel to be replaced in the units from which it had been withdrawn, the Field Marshal Commanding-in-Chief recommended in May, 1918, that Field Survey units in Armies should be organized as battalions, each under the command of a Lieutenant-Colonel, with an Adjutant. This was approved, and each Battalion organized as follows :—

- 1 Headquarter Section,
- 2 Artillery Sections,
- Corps Topographical Section.

The Headquarter Section to deal with surveying, compilation and printing, each Artillery Section to consist of Sound-Ranging Sections and Observation Groups. Units were placed for tactical purposes under the direct control of G.O.C.s, R.A., of Armies, who detailed tasks to be performed.

Four Field Survey Battalions were formed for the 1st, 2nd, 3rd and 4th Armies. In addition there was a Headquarter Section for the 5th Army, and three Sound-Ranging Sections were formed in France in readiness for service in other theatres of war. The Depôt Field Survey Company was also organized into a Battalion under a Lieutenant-Colonel. Small additions were made to the establishment of the Headquarter Section and School for Observers to provide for the survey of back areas and to supply reinforcements to the other battalions.

When the Depôt Field Survey Company was first formed, the Printing Company was absorbed into it as a Printing Section. This was found to be unsatisfactory, and when reorganization on a Battalion basis took place, the Printing Section was restored to its original status as a Printing Company, R.E. The above reorganization resulted in a net increase in personnel of 82 officers and 603 other ranks, in addition to which one Topographical Section, consisting of four officers and 48 other ranks, was added to the Depôt Field Survey Battalion.

Anti-Aircraft Organization (Home).

In December, 1915, it became apparent that Anti-Aircraft Searchlights were required for Home Defence purposes. To man them, A.A. Searchlight Companies were raised as part of the Territorial Force. The greater number were provided by the London and Tyne Electrical Engineers, the remainder by various Fortress, R.E. (T.F.) companies, such as the Hants, Kent, Essex, etc. The number of units constantly increased, as Anti-Aircraft Defence developed, until, in July, 1917, there were 42 units scattered about the country. In November, 1917, the A.A. Defences of Great Britain were reorganized. The A.A. Companies, R.E., were reduced to 12 and personnel was attached to 59 A.A. Companies, R.G.A., to run the lights working in conjunction with their guns. The London and Tyne Electrical Engineers became the parent units of all R.E. A.A. personnel in Great Britain, and undertook all their training, etc. By November, 1918, the number of A.A. Companies, R.E., had increased to 17, and there were about 56 A.A. Companies, R.G.A., with R.E. attached.

Anti-Aircraft Organization (Overseas).

In March, 1915, the Field Marshal Commanding-in-Chief in France asked for three or four searchlights suitable for use with Anti-Aircraft guns against Airship attack by night. No. 1 Anti-Aircraft Section— one officer and 19 other ranks, with three lights—was accordingly formed at Chatham and embarked in April. Another section was then asked for, as it was considered that one was required at Boulogne and one at G.H.Q. No. 2 Section was accordingly formed at Plymouth and embarked in July.

In August, 1917, it was estimated that at least 30 additional Anti-Aircraft Searchlight Sections would be required in France. Personnel for new sections was accordingly provided, partly by the withdrawal of men from A.A. and Coast Defence Searchlights in the United Kingdom. This personnel was sent to France in drafts and there formed into sections. In January, 1918, one section was sent from France to Italy. The number of sections then serving overseas was :

In France, 1 to 33, 35 to 49, 51 to 77 = 75 Sections
In Italy, 34 ... ... = 1 Section

Total ... ... 76 Sections.

In June, 1918, the Field Marshal Commanding-in-Chief in France asked for the A.A. Searchlight Establishment to be raised to 285 lights, organized in 95 sections of three lights each. Four sections were formed of Canadian personnel and were called the Canadian A.A. Searchlight Company. Personnel to bring the existing sections —which were two-light sections—up to three-light sections, was sent to France in October, 1918, and steps were taken to form the 16 extra sections required, but owing to the cessation of hostilities they were not actually formed.

Further details will be found later in this volume under the heading " Anti-Aircraft Searchlights."

Emergency Sections.

The 1st and 2nd London Demolition Sections were formed from the London Reserve Field Companies, R.E. (T.F.) in the summer of 1917, to deal with damage caused to buildings in London by enemy aircraft. Two additional sections were formed later from troops under the G.H.Q., Home Forces.

An establishment of two officers and 92 other ranks for these sections was approved in March, 1918, and their designation was changed to Emergency Sections.

Chapter IV.

WORKS COMPANIES, FORESTRY UNITS, ARMY TRAMWAY AND FOREWAY COMPANIES, INUNDATION SECTION, CAMOUFLAGE PARK, METEOROLOGICAL SECTIONS, REINFORCEMENT COMPANIES, COAST DEFENCE UNITS, ENGINEER SERVICES.

Works Companies.

At a conference held at the War Office in July, 1918, it was decided to send to France six Works Companies for work on aerodrome construction for the R.A.F. The Companies selected were:—

6th Works Company (Regular)
22nd Works Company (Regular)
39th Works Company (Regular)
575th (Hants) Works Company (T.F.)
563rd (Hants) Works Company (T.F.)
572nd (Devon) Works Company (T.F.)

The 578th (Sussex) Works Company was subsequently substituted for the 563rd (Hants) Works Company. The Works Companies were sent overseas in August and September, 1918, and were replaced at their respective Home Stations by Field Companies drawn from Home Service Divisions and Mixed Brigades. The establishment at which the Works Companies embarked was three officers and 92 other ranks. Ten other Works Companies were employed under the Director of Fortifications and Works in Commands at Home.

Water Companies

In the spring of 1917 a Company designated the 360th Water Supply Company, R.E., was formed in Egypt for the installation and maintenance of water supply plant in that country. Its establishment was five officers and 158 other ranks. In September, 1917, a second Water Supply Company—the 359th—was formed at the same establishment, and in February, 1918, a third—the 357th—was formed with an establishment of eight officers and 197 other ranks.

Workshop Companies.

In the early days of trench warfare a number of R.E. shops were organized in France to provide extemporized grenades, trench mortars and trench stores of various descriptions.

In June, 1917, the Field Marshal Commanding-in-Chief British Armies in France recommended that, with a view to regularizing the employment of the personnel in these shops, a definite establishment for an Army R.E. Workshop should be approved. In July, 1917, an establishment of seven officers and 124 other ranks was approved accordingly, and five units formed. Each consisted of a headquarters and four sections, each of which was organized so that it could, if necessary, be detached to work with a Corps. The personnel was obtained from the R.E. Reinforcement Companies in France. The final designation of these units was Nos. 1, 2, 3, 4 and 5, Army Workshop Companies. (Further details will be found in the section of this volume headed " Machinery, Workshops and Electricity.")

Artisan Works Companies.

In April, 1916, the Field Marshal Commanding-in-Chief in France recommended the provision of 2,100 skilled and 13,950 unskilled men for work in connection with road making, hutting, timber cutting, quarrying and the loading and unloading of ships and railway wagons. Six hundred of the skilled men were required for road making and hutting. To supply the requirement, men over military age and under 50 were sent out in drafts from England and formed overseas into the 51st, 52nd, 58th and 60th Artisan Works Companies, each of a strength of three officers and 147 other ranks. The men were paid ordinary R.E. rates. Difficulty was experienced in obtaining the necessary numbers of men by direct enlistment, and it became necessary to make them up by sending out Category B1 men from Home units.

In February, 1918, the five Area Employment (Artisan R.E.) Companies of the Labour Corps in France were transferred to the R.E. and became the 240th, 241st, 242nd, 243rd and 244th Artisan Works Companies. Five more Artisan Works Companies were formed in France and were designated the 1501st, 1502nd, 1503rd, 1504th and 1505th.

Forestry Units.

In February, 1917, the War Office took over the control of forestry operations in France, and in March, 1917, an establishment for a Directorate of Forestry in France was approved, and it was decided that this Directorate should be a Royal Engineer Directorate. In May, 1917, establishments—submitted by the authorities in France for the undermentioned units—were approved :—

Army Area Forestry Group (including H.Q. and Forestry Control),
Lines of Communication Forestry Group (including H.Q. of Groups
    and Forest Districts),
Forestry Companies. R.E.

The establishment of a Forestry Company was four officers and 110 other ranks. Eleven were formed and allotted the numbers from 361 to 371 inclusive. Two Artisan Works Companies were also formed for forestry work.

Army Tramway Companies and Foreway Companies.

In April, 1917, it was notified from France that it had been found necessary to form a number of Army Tramway Companies, R.E., to construct, maintain and operate the trench tramway systems in advance of the light railways. The establishment recommended was three officers and 103 other ranks per company and, in addition, one officer and one corporal attached to each Army H.Q. Seven companies had been formed, and two more were in process of formation, the personnel being obtained from R.E. Labour Battalions and other R.E. units. Covering approval was requested for the formation of the above companies. This was given, and the units designated the 372nd to 380th Army Tramways Companies, R.E.

In March, 1918, the Field Marshal Commanding-in-Chief British Armies in France proposed to organize a new service for the detailed distribution of ammunition, stores and supplies beyond the point to which normal railway services went—this service was called the "Foreways," the term Tramways being superseded. The new organization was to absorb all existing Tramway Units and certain other personnel. It was proposed to form 16 Company H.Q. and 22 Construction and Operating sections, the personnel being found from the following :—

> 9 Army Tramway Companies,
> 31st Army Troops Company,
> Reduction of four men in each Field Company,
> 1 additional Army Troops Company.

Owing to the increases involved in these proposals they were not sanctioned, and a fresh scheme was asked for, involving no additional personnel. The nine Tramway Companies and the 31st Army Troops Company were, however, renamed Nos. 1 to 10 Foreway Companies. About the middle of 1918 the Foreway organization was transferred to the Directorate of Light Railways, and these units became "Transportation" R.E. Units. (Further details are given in the section of this volume entitled "Forward Communications.")

Inundation Sections.

As an outcome of a request by the Army Council, the President of the Institution of Civil Engineers appointed a Committee to report on a proposed scheme of inundation in France. This Committee presented their report in May, 1918, and, in order to carry out their suggestions, an Inundation Section, strength :

      6 Surveyors (junior officers),
     12 other ranks (with survey experience),

was sent out. One captain and one batman were afterwards added to the above establishment. (*See also* section of this volume entitled " Inundations.")

CAMOUFLAGE PARK.

In May, 1916, a Special Works Park, consisting of seven officers and 82 other ranks, was formed for Camouflage work in France. In April, 1917, its establishment was increased to 28 officers and 315 other ranks, and in May, 1917, to 30 officers and 316 other ranks. Owing to the growing importance of camouflage work the establishment was further increased later to 58 officers and 346 other ranks. In November, 1918, the Park was organized into a Headquarters of five officers and five other ranks, and Army Camouflage Factories each of two officers and 26 other ranks.

In addition to the Special Works Park in France, a Special Works School for experimental and instructional purposes was formed in England.

The titles of the two establishments were changed to Camouflage Park and Camouflage School in July, 1918. (*See also* section of this volume entitled " Camouflage.")

METEOROLOGICAL SECTIONS.

A Meteorological Section was first formed for France, and subsequently sections were approved for Salonika and Egypt. Personnel for these sections was in the first place found from the staff of the Civil Meteorological Office. Subsequently this source could not provide all the men wanted, as, owing to the requirements of the Air Force and Special Brigade, a largely increased meteorological service became necessary. Men of sufficient education were then transferred to R.E. from other arms, or were specially enlisted and trained. In March, 1918, an establishment was drawn up for a Meteorological Section (Home), and this unit performed the dual functions of training men for drafts and supplying meteorological information for home purposes. At the same time all meteorological services at home and abroad were put under one Commandant. During November, 1918, a small Meteorological Section was formed for service in North Russia.

REINFORCEMENT COMPANIES.

In order to utilize R.E. reinforcements in France prior to their absorption in units, the Field Marshal Commanding-in-Chief notified in January, 1917, that arrangements had been made to form, as a temporary measure, certain R.E. Reinforcement Companies for work in Army Areas, and asked that authority might be given for the formation of any number of companies up to eight, with the following Headquarter establishment :

> 1 Captain,
> 1 Subaltern,
> 1 Company-Sergeant-Major,
> 1 Company-Quartermaster-Sergeant.

Approval was given in February, 1917.

In March, 1917, the Field Marshal Commanding-in-Chief asked for authority to form further Reinforcement Companies, as and when trained R.E. reinforcements became available. It was pointed out that all companies so formed would be employed in Army Areas where they would be conveniently placed for reinforcing other R.E. units as required. This proposal was also approved.

In September, 1917, the situation became such that it was expedient to withdraw all reinforcements from R.E. Reinforcement Companies in Army Areas and orders were accordingly issued for these companies to be broken up.

Coast Defence Units.

It has already been stated (in Chapter I) that at the outbreak of war 11 Fortress Companies for Coast Defence existed at home and 15 abroad. Some were entirely for electric light duty, and some for both electric light and works duties. On mobilization the duties of these units were partially taken over by the Territorial Force, as far as those at home stations were concerned. As a rule, the Regular Companies were not entirely withdrawn from the defences. Personnel in them, fit for service abroad, were, however, gradually replaced by men unfit for such service. The units withdrawn from Coast Defence work at home and abroad were as follows :—

> 1st Company, Gibraltar, converted into an Advanced Park Company for France.
> 4th Company, Gosport, converted into an Advanced Park Company for Salonika.
> 24th Company, Malta, converted into a Base Park Company for France.
> 32nd Company, Gibraltar, converted into a Base Park Company for France.
> 33rd Company, Cork, converted into a Base Park Company for Salonika.
> 47th Company, Capetown, converted into a Base Park Company for Mesopotamia.

The 1/1st Devon Works Company (afterwards the 567th Army Troops Company) embarked for Gibraltar in December, 1914, to replace the 32nd Company. It was relieved at Gibraltar in the spring of 1915 by the 1/2nd Devon Works Company (afterwards the 568th Army Troops Company). This latter Company was relieved by the 1/5th Glamorgan Works Company (afterwards the 558th Works Company) in November, 1916. The 1st Company was replaced at Gibraltar by the 1/4th Devon E.L. Company (afterwards the 614th Fortress Company). The former unit left Gibraltar in April, 1915, and the latter unit remained there till the end of the war.

Development of Coast Defence Organization at Home.

As stated above, the Coast Defence work of the United Kingdom was largely taken over by the Territorial Force early in the war. The raising of 2nd Line T.F. units was authorized in June, 1916. In August, 1917, there were no less than 47 E.L. and 17 Works Companies, T.F., in addition to two Coast Works Companies (*see* below) and 12 Fortress Companies (Regulars). It was realized that this organization was extravagant in personnel and after much discussion the Coast Defence units were reorganized on a basis of eight men per light, and an establishment was issued in August, 1918. The new organization consisted of Fortress Companies and Fortress Works Companies. In garrisons where there were no Fortress Works Companies the Fortress Companies were in some cases composed of an E.L. Section, a Signal Section and a Works Section, in others of E.L. and Works Sections or even of an E.L. Section alone. Where there was a Fortress Works Company in the garrison, the Fortress Company had no Works Section. In a few cases where there were no Works personnel, Works Companies were allotted to Commands independently of garrisons. The saving effected by this reorganization was 151 officers and 2433 other ranks.

At the same time the H.Q. of the Tyne E.E. and London E.E. became the parent units for all Coast Defence and Anti-Aircraft Electric Light units and the Reserve Depôts for training all E.L. personnel, thus rendering it possible to close down other Territorial Headquarters and Depôts. Owing, however, to the cessation of hostilities, the closing down of these Depôts was suspended in December, 1918.

Coast Battalion Companies.

Two of these units existed in 1914 (the 16th and 49th Companies), split up into sections for Coast Defence work in the Northern and Scottish Commands On the reorganization of the Coast Defences in 1918, they became Fortress Works Companies in the Tyne and Forth garrisons respectively.

COAST WORKS COMPANIES.

Two of these units were formed at the Humber in June, 1916, from personnel for Coast Garrisons at home, fit for home service only. They were designated the 168th and 169th Coast Works Companies, and the establishment of each was five officers and 209 other ranks. They were disbanded in November, 1917.

ESTABLISHMENT FOR ENGINEER SERVICES.

Immediately prior to the War the supervising and clerical establishment for Engineer Services at home and abroad consisted of :—

Military—

Superintending Inspectors of Works and Inspectors of Works	48
Foremen of Works ...	269
Engineer Clerks, Draughtsmen and Ledgerkeepers	250
Military Mechanists (Machinery) and Electricians	213
Total Military	780

Civilian—

Temporary Surveyors' Clerks, Clerks of Works, Pensioner Foremen of Works, Clerks, Draughtsmen and Ledgerkeepers ...	398
Grand Total ...	1178

A considerable number of the Military Staff were detailed to proceed overseas with the Expeditionary Force to France, but further heavy demands had to be met almost immediately, and these were drawn from the Home Commands, their places being filled by appointing civilians.

Before the end of 1914 it became necessary to provide officers for Works duties with the Expeditionary Forces, in order to release officers, R.E., for duties in the Field, and to meet this a new grade, called Temporary Inspectors of Works, was introduced, with the rank of Lieutenant.

These officers were appointed from lists of Civil Engineers who had a knowledge of the French language.

A large number of these officers were appointed from time to time and sent overseas, to meet demands as they arrived, and were also posted to home stations as Division Officers and Assistant Division Officers in order to release Royal Engineer officers.

Four Roads Officers were appointed in December, 1914, for the Eastern, Southern, and Northern Commands and Central Force respectively. They were afterwards absorbed into the Lands Branch.

Early in 1915, a demand for surveyors' clerks was met by selecting a number of Military Foremen of Works who possessed all the necessary qualifications, and sending them to France, there being no military personnel graded as surveyors' clerks.

It soon became necessary to augment the permanent military establishment by the formation of a temporary establishment, and the personnel for this was found from the Corps, in the case of clerks, draughtsmen and ledgerkeepers, by men of low category.

In April, 1915, the supply of clerks and ledgerkeepers could not be maintained in that manner, and it became necessary to specially enlist men, giving them the rank of Corporal. This, however, was discontinued as soon as the necessary men were obtained from the Corps.

In May, 1915, appeals were sent to all foreign stations, asking that any warrant officers or non-commissioned officers who could be spared might be sent home to assist in providing for requirements.

A demand from France for officers specially qualified for duties in connection with shipping and stores was met by selecting and commissioning men with the rank of 2nd-Lieutenant on the General List.

By the end of the War the strength of the personnel employed as Engineer Services had risen to the following:—

Military—
Expeditionary Forces	1510
Colonial Stations	134
Home	781
Total Military	**2425**

Civilian—
Colonial Stations	356
Home Stations	3485
	3841

CHAPTER V.

TRANSPORTATION UNITS, ETC.

TRANSPORTATION UNITS AND PERSONNEL.

Transportation Services include Railways, Roads, Inland Water Transport and Docks. Personnel for these services was provided on the same lines as for the remainder of the Royal Engineers up to September, 1916. A Director-General of Transportation, controlling all these services, was then appointed, and the administration of Transportation units and personnel was thereafter carried out by branches under his control.

RAILWAY UNITS.

In August, 1914, there were two Regular (8th and 10th) and three Special Reserve (one Royal Anglesey R.E. and two Royal Monmouth R.E.) Railway Companies. Their establishments were as follows :—

	Officers.	Other ranks.
8th Railway Company	3	106
10th Railway Company	3	106
Depôt	2	4
Royal Anglesey R.E. (1 Company)	5	145
Royal Monmouth R.E. (2 Companies)	10	290
Total	23	651

The 8th Railway Company landed in France in August, 1914, and the 10th and two Special Reserve Companies in November. The third Special Reserve Company landed in February, 1915.

A Railway Transport Section was also formed from Regular sources for service in France.

It was soon seen that the above units would not suffice for probable requirements, and the Director of Railway Transport was instructed to organize additional Railway Construction units. In October, 1914, the Railway Executive Committee in England formed a Sub-Committee for Recruiting. Very large numbers of the employees of British Railway Companies were then volunteering for military service, and the men for Railway units were selected from them. By the end of 1917, out of some 180,000 enlistments from English Railway Companies, about 40,000 men, were serving in Railway units.

Approximately half the officers for the new units were provided by the British Railway Companies on the recommendation of the Railway Executive Committee and the other half were mainly men from overseas who had been employed on colonial and foreign railways.

In the Italian theatre of war the railways—other than light railways—were entirely operated and maintained by the Italian authorities, but in other theatres of war the railways were run by personnel under the Transportation Directorate.

In the Salonika theatre three Construction and three Operating Companies were employed, and large numbers of Greeks, Egyptians and Turkish prisoners were employed as civil labour. In Egypt and Palestine there were five Construction and eighteen Operating Companies, and much native labour was also used.

Road Units.

Road and Quarry Companies were only formed for the French theatre of war. At the end of 1916 the necessity for their formation became apparent. Officers were selected on the recommendation of the Road Board from lists submitted by them, comprising some 1,300 serving officers and 1,300 civilians. Units formed by counties and county boroughs were officered as far as possible by local men, who were given rank suitable to their technical qualifications, subject to at least one trained officer joining each company as a transfer. At a conference convened by the Director of Roads it was decided that the more important counties and county boroughs should raise the men for complete companies, 250 strong, while those with smaller populations should combine to form companies. As regards the formation of Quarry Companies, quarry officials and masters in the British Isles were approached, and, as a result, 10 companies were formed in Great Britain and one in Ireland. Two more companies were formed by transfers in France.

Light Railway Units.

It was not till towards the end of 1916 that any great development of the light railways in France took place. The adoption of an extended system was then decided on. Thenceforward the personnel employed on light railways increased very largely, and, by the end of the War, there were some thirty Light Railway Companies of various descriptions in France.

In Italy the Italian authorities could not provide any personnel for light railways. One Light Railway Operating Company was therefore sent to this theatre of war early in 1918.

Considerable use of light railways was made in Salonika and in Egypt and Palestine, and two Light Railway Operating Companies were employed in each of these theatres.

Inland Water Transport and Docks Personnel.

The Inland Water Transport and Docks Section of the Royal Engineers was originally formed in December, 1914, to deal with and develop transport on the canals and waterways of France and Belgium. The Section at first operated under the Director of Railways, but, owing to the rapid development of Inland Water Transport, a special Directorate was formed in October, 1915.

In the summer of 1916 all non-transport work in Mesopotamia became a part of the Inland Water Transport Directorate's responsibilities, and during 1917 its scope was extended to cover Inland Water Transport and Dock Working in Egypt, in Salonika, and in other theatres of war.

This entailed large increases in establishments, and, up to December, 1917, some 1,100 officers and nearly 30,000 men were transferred to or enlisted in the Inland Water Transport Section. During 1917 over 600 officers and 8,000 men were drafted overseas to theatres of war as under:—

	Officers.	Other ranks.
France	87	5787
Mesopotamia	465	1394
Salonika	12	171
Mediterranean L. of C.	34	697
Egypt	29	94
East Africa	6	127
Total	633	8270

The European personnel in Mesopotamia was supplemented by over 42,000 natives of India, Egyptians, West Africans and Chinese.

At the cessation of hostilities the total Inland Water Transport and Docks personnel amounted to 1,666 officers and 29,436 other ranks.

Depôts and Training Centres.

The Headquarters of the Regular railway troops before the War was at Longmoor, and the Special Reserve Companies came there annually for training.

During the War Longmoor and subsequently part of Bordon became the centre for all railway and road personnel, and at one time also for inland water transport personnel. From the outbreak of the War till the end of November, 1918, nearly 1,700 officers and 66,000 other ranks were sent overseas from this centre, including 30 officers and 3,000 other ranks for Colonial Transportation Units.

For Quarry units a special Depôt was formed at Buxton.

After the base of the Inland Water Transport was moved from Dover to Richborough, the depôt for personnel was established at Sandwich.

Final Strength of Transportation Personnel.

At the end of 1918 the personnel, provided under the supervision of the Transportation Directorate and employed on Railways, Inland Waterways and Roads, numbered the following :—

Raised in England	62,344
Colonial Corps sent from England	22,608
Units raised overseas	23,390
Grand total, all ranks	108,342

The units in which this personnel was serving and its distribution is shown in the statement which follows :—

ORDER OF BATTLE OF R.E. UNITS IN ALL THEATRES ON 11TH NOVEMBER, 1918.
(R.E. RAILWAY AND ROAD TROOPS.)

Unit.	Home.	France.	Italy.	Egypt.	Salonika.	East Africa.
Depôts.	R.E. Railway Construction Troops Depôt. R.E. Railway Operating Troops Depôt. R.E. Road and Quarry Troops Depôt. H.Q. Railways and Roads Training Centre.	D.G.T. Base Depôt.			Base Depôt.	
Military Railways at Home.	Military Camp Railways. Woolmer Instructional Military Railway.					
R.E. Railway Construction Cos.		8, 10, 109 to 114, 118, 119, 120, 259 to 264, 268, 296, 271, 275, 277, 278, 279, 280, 281, 282, 295 to 298. No. 3 R.A.R.E. (S.R.) Nos. 2 and 3, R.M.R.E. (S.R.)		115, 116, 265, 266, 272	117, 273, 267	
Railway Survey and Reconnaissance Sections		1 to 7		106	108	
Railway Signal and Interlocking Co.		200				
Wagon Erecting Cos.		16, 17, 18, 66, 67, 70	One Sect.			
Broad Gauge Workshop Cos.		61, 62, 63, 78, 79, 80				
Broad Gauge Miscellaneous Trades Cos.		37, 38, 39, 82, 83				
Electrical Sections.		1, 2, 3				

ORDER OF BATTLE OF R.E. UNITS IN ALL THEATRES ON 11TH NOVEMBER, 1918.—*Cont.*

(R.E. RAILWAY AND ROAD TROOPS.)

Unit.	Home.	France.	Italy.	Egypt.	Salonika.	East Africa
Headquarters Sects. with A. D. L.R.		1 to 5				
Light Railway Operating Cos.		1, 2, 4, 6, 10, 11, 29 to 34	109 (one platoon only).	96, 203	107, 33	
Light Railway Train Crew Cos.		18 to 22		98		
Light Railway Forward Cos.		231, 232, 234 to 240				
Light Railway Miscellaneous Trades Cos.		23, 24				
Light Railway Workshop Cos.		25, 26				
Light Railway Tractor Repair Co.		28				
Training Schools.		Light Railway Training School. Light Railway (Forward) Training School. R.O.D. Training School.				
Railway Traffic Sections.		1 to 13 Two Railway Traffic Sections. (Medn. L. of C.).	Three Sections. (not numbered).	Five Sections (not numbered).	No. 1	
Broad Gauge Operating Companies.		1 to 7, 9, 11 to 15, 20 to 31, 34, 40 to 53, 64, 65		71 to 77, 94, 95, 99 to 105, 201 202	19, 32, 204	

ORDER OF BATTLE OF R.E. UNITS IN ALL THEATRES ON 11TH NOVEMBER, 1918.—Cont.

(R.E. RAILWAY AND ROAD TROOPS.)

Unit.	Home.	France.	Italy.	Egypt.	Salonika.	East Africa.
Road Construction Companies.		301 to 319, 330 to 347, 349				391, 392 (nuclei only).
Quarry Companies.		198, 199, 320 to 329, 348				
Quarry Maintenance Section.		1				
Steam Boiler Repair Company.		Not numbered.				
Transportation Stores Companies.	R.E. Transportation Stores Company, Purfleet.	1 to 13	Stores Section.		Stores Park 270	
Railway Labour Company.						

ORDER OF BATTLE I.W. & D.

Unit.	Home.	France.	Mesopotamia.	Egypt.	Italy.
Depôts.	H.Q. Richborough. H.Q. Southampton. H.Q. Poplar. H.Q. Richborough Depôt (Richborough). Sanitary Establishment. Depôt Companies, 1—6 (Richborough.)	I.W.T., H.Q. Sections, 1—16, 24—27. B.E.F. Common to Army Areas and the Lines of Communication. H.Q. of O.C. I.W.T. Troops located at Aire. *Docks:* No. 1 H.Q. Boulogne. No. 2 H.Q. Havre.	Following at Basra:—H.Q., I.W.T. Depôt Headquarters of following formations:—Vessels, Marine Engineering, Accounts, Dockyards and Shipbuilding, Native Craft, I.W.T. Stores, Buoyage and Pilotage. Conservancy and Reclamation, Camps, Coal Depôt, Barge Depôt, H.Q. Construction (Baghdad), H.Q. Construction (Euphrates).	Cairo, Sections at Port Said, Kantara Ferry, Suez, Port Alexandria, Ismailia, Kerch and Assonar, Behera, Assiout, Menufer, Girga, Minia, Mansourah.	M.L.O.C. Taranto.
Workshop and Shipyard Companies.	H.Q. Richborough, 11—17 Richborough, 19—27 Richborough, 37—40 Richborough, 43—48 Richborough.				

ORDER OF BATTLE I.W. & D.—Cont.

Unit.	Home.	France.	Mesopotamia.	East Africa. Egypt.
Construction Companies.	H.Q. Richborough, 96, 97 Richborough, 98 Poole, 99 Southampton, 100—103 Manston, 104 Poole, 105 Hawkings, 106—108 Amesbury, 109 Lulworth, 116 Poole, 117, 118 Richborough, 119 Slough, 120 Farlington, 121 Amesbury, 122 Poole, 131, 132 Richborough, 136 Richborough, 141, 142 Richborough.	*Docks.*—*Cont.*: No. 4 H.Q. Calais. No. 5 H.Q. Dunkirk. No. 6 H.Q. Dieppe. Docks, Cherbourg. No. 8 P.C. Co. R.E., Boulogne. No. 11 P.C. Co. R.E., Havre. *Port Construction Cos.*: C.E.P.C., H.Q. D.G.T. G.H.Q. No. 1 P.C. H.Q. Dunkirk. No. 2 P.C. H.Q., Rangde-Fliers. No. 3 P.C. H.Q. Oissel-Rouen. No. 1 P.C. Co., Lery. No. 2 P.C. Co., Quevilly-Rouen. No. 6 P.C. Co., Oissel-Rouen. No. 4 P.C. Co., Rang-de-Fliers. No. 5 P.C. Co., Les Forts-Bergues. No. 6 P.C. Co., Dunkirk. No. 7 P.C. Co. Ostend.	DETACHMENTS AT THE FOLLOWING PLACES:— *Camps*: Margil, Khora Creek, Tancoma (Abadan). NARROW SECTION: Ezra's Tomb Gumaijah Shargi South Station, Michriya C. Stn. Central Stn. Quadat Saleh, Majar Kahir, North Station, Ali Charbi, Sumar. BAGHDAD SECTIONS:— Zeur, Hinaidi, Advanced Base, Baghdad, Sadieyeh, Akab, Samarrah, Diala, Baguaba. *Persian Lines of Communication*: Karun, Ahwaz, Muscat. UPPER EUPHRATES: I.O.V. and I.M.E. Dhibban, Riverhead, Hit, Ramadie, Madij, Abu Huyat, Uqbah, Feluja, I.W.T.O. MIDDLE EUPHRATES: Hillah, Iseurieriyen, Musayib, Tawerij, Kufa, Hindia, Barrage,Magranal Delha and El Hassam, Jebeira. Madhetia, Jerboyian, Zenafiah, Daghara, Jellan, Afaij, Ebra, Khan, Jadwal, Diwanieh, Imam Hamzah, Rumetha, Hamadieh, Gus, Kifl, Shamiyeh, Chemas, Abu Sakair, Kala Abasiyah. LOWER EUPHRATES: Durraji, Sarnawah, Nasseriyeh, Waar, Shenafiah.	Port Amelia, Mozambique, Lindi, Dares-Salaam, Kilindini.
Marine Companies.	H.Q. Richborough, 70—75 Richborough, 76 Poplar.			Russia. Murmansk.
Traffic Companies.	H.Q. Richborough, 56—61 Richborough.			
Train Ferry Companies.	H.Q. Richborough, 85, 86 Richborough, 87, 88 Southampton.			
T.F. Shore Company.	62 Southampton.			
Stores Companies.	H.Q. Richborough, 90—91 Richborough.			
Accounts Company.	95 Richborough.			
Mesopotamia Reserve Unit.	Glasgow.			
Marine Company (Scottish Canal).	144 Glasgow.			
Craft Repair Company.	77 Poplar.			
Home Depôt.	Richborough.			
Tugmasters.	Richborough.			

CHAPTER VI.

ARMY POSTAL SERVICES.

AT the outbreak of war the Postal Services personnel for the Expeditionary Force was supplied from a Postal Section of the Royal Engineers (Special Reserve) composed entirely of G.P.O. staff and employees.

The authorized establishment was 10 officers, 40 warrant officers and serjeants, and 250 rank and file. Total, 300. This establishment was intended both to supply the personnel for the B.E.F. and to meet the wastages of a normal campaign.

As the size of the Army increased and new theatres of war came into being, it was found necessary to form a home Postal Depôt, both to act as a draft-finding unit and to handle the mails for all theatres of war. The Headquarters of the Depôt was at the G.P.O. and the personnel was drawn from amongst P.O. employees enlisted for the duration of the War.

It was decided in 1917 not to enlist any more men into the Postal Service, R.E.S.R., but to post them instead to the London Regiment and attach them to the Postal Service for duty—thus preventing men so enlisted from drawing Engineer pay in the army, in addition to their full civil pay. A Postal Company of the 8th Battalion, London Regiment, was therefore formed, which was merged later into the Home Postal Depôt. The establishment of the Depôt was fixed in July, 1918, at 15 officers, 72 warrant officers and serjeants, 1,113 other ranks, 140 civilians (ex-soldiers), and 1,120 women. The rank and file included a minimum of 250 men belonging to the Postal Company, who supplied drafts to theatres of war. The remaining R.E. personnel included in this total were intended to be gradually replaced by women in the proportion of three to two, down to a workable minimum, and also sent overseas.

In September, 1914, it was decided to form an Army Postal Service, T.F., for the troops stationed at home.

In February, 1916, the D.A.P.S. (Home) recommended a reduction in the postal personnel allotted to formations at home. The reason given for this recommendation was the suspension of the parcel post, etc. Reduced establishments were accordingly approved in April, 1917.

The Home Army Postal Service underwent modifications from time to time in conformity with the changes in the formations considered necessary to be retained for home defence. In October, 1918, a nucleus establishment was laid down for normal working at home, which could be expanded in the event of an invasion or other grave emergency. The personnel to provide the expanded establishment was to be found from the Home Postal Depôt.

In October, 1918, the Director of Army Postal Services at home recommended the formation of a London Volunteer Postal Company, the object being to supplement the Postal Service at home in the event of an emergency, as the Home Depôt, on account of the number of women who were being absorbed into the establishment, would be unable to find sufficient personnel. This unit was organized on an R.E. basis. Its personnel was drawn from men exempted from Army service and from men in the London Postal Service who were over the age fixed for liability for military service under the Military Service Acts.

Postal Service in France.

The postal personnel required for the Expeditionary Force of 1914 was laid down in *War Establishments Part I.*, 1914. The growth of this service was in proportion to the growth of the Armies generally, and as the number of Divisions overseas increased, so automatically did the Postal Service. Early in the War it was arranged that, as each new Division was sent to France, an allotment of 11 other ranks postal personnel was despatched to deal with the corresponding increase in postal traffic on the L. of C.

In April, 1917, the Field Marshal Commanding-in-Chief notified that the allotment of 11 all ranks for each British Division would not suffice to cope with the expected increase of extra-Divisional units, especially in those controlled by the Director of Transportation. It was therefore recommended that the necessary steps be taken to enlist in the R.E. Postal Service a sufficient number of men to raise the Divisional allotment from a total of 11 to 13 all ranks.

The War Office, in a letter dated 27th May, 1917, informed France that no more men could be spared for employment on postal work on L. of C., and suggested that women be employed. France replied that as it would take some time to train women, men should be sent, and asked that 55 men be sent as early as possible. These were sent during June and July.

In February, 1918, the Field Marshal Commanding-in-Chief, France, forwarded proposals for the reorganization of the Postal Services in France, and stated that the method of basing the allotment of postal personnel on the number of Divisions in the country was not satisfactory, owing to the large number of units in the country, such as R.G.A. Batteries, Flying Corps units, Labour and Transportation units, etc., the allotment of 11 men per Division did not furnish an adequate number to provide a satisfactory Postal Service, and he suggested that the most satisfactory scale on which to base the allotment of Postal Service personnel was the total number of troops in the country. He also asked sanction for the attachment of 150 low-category men to meet the expansion in the L. of C. area.

These proposals in brief were :—

(1) The formation of an Auxiliary Postal Company.
(2) Alteration in the establishment of the four Base Post Offices already in existence at Boulogne, Calais, Havre and Rouen.
(3) Employment of Q.M.A.A.C.s in place of men in the new Auxiliary Postal Company.
(4) Sanctioning of employment of " attached " men of low-medical category on the L. of C.

These proposals were approved with some very slight amendments, and are shown in the attached Table A. :—

Table A.

Postal Units.	R.E. Postal Personnel.					Q.M.A.A.C.s.			Attd. low Medical Category Men.	Remarks.
	Officers.	W.O.s	Serjeants.	Other N.C.O.s and Men.	Total, Other Ranks.	Forewomen.	Other Ranks.	Total.	Other Ranks.	
Auxiliary Postal Company*	7	18	42	613	673	6	94	100	90	*This establishment was based on the strength of troops in France as on 1/12/17 calculated on a scale of 9 postal men per 20,000 in the country. For every 50,000 troops above or below the number as on 1/12/17 the establishment was increased or decreased by 10 O.R., Indian, Chinese, etc., being counted for this purpose as one quarter of their actual number.
4 Base P.O.s	16	12	16	224	252	4	84	88	60	
Cavalry Corps H.Q. and 15 Corps H.Q. (1 Imperial Corps has Overseas Postal personnel)					16					
Grand Total	23	30	58	837	941	10	178	188	150	

which replaced the former Establishments.

Divisional allotment	6	12	25	557	594					49 Divisions at 11 men per Division = 539
Four Base P.O.s	16	12	16	272	300					55 men sent out in June and July, 1917 ... ... = 55
Cavalry Corps and 15 Corps H.Q. Clerks to D.A.D.A. P.S.					16					
Grand Total	22	24	41	829	910					Total 594

The establishment of postal officers in France in November, 1918, was:—

At G.H.Q.—
- 1 D. of A.P.S., Lieut.-Colonel—Acting Brig.-General, but without pay and allowances of acting rank.
- 3 A.D. of A.P.S., Captains—Acting Lieut.-Colonels, but without pay and allowances of acting rank.
- 1 D.A.D. of A.P.S., Lieutenant—Acting Major, but without pay and allowances of acting rank.

On L. of C.—
- 2 D.D. of A.P.S., Majors or Lieut.-Colonels—Acting Colonels, but without pay and allowances of acting rank.
- 4 A.D. of A.P.S. for Base Ports, Captains—Acting Lieut.-Colonels, but without pay and allowances for acting rank.
- 1 A.D. of A.P.S. L. of C. (North), Captain—Acting Lieut.-Colonel, but without pay and allowances of acting rank.
- 1 D.A.D. of A.P.S. L. of C. (North), Lieutenant—Acting Major, but without pay and allowances of acting rank.
- 1 D.A.D. of A.P.S. L. of C. (South), Lieutenant—Acting Major, but without pay and allowances of acting rank.

And in addition 1 D.A.D. of A.P.S. to each Army and Corps.

RANKS AND PAY OF POSTAL SERVICE OFFICERS.

It was decided very early in the War that it was inexpedient to pay Army Postal officers on a scale corresponding to their necessary military status, as they drew their full civil pay from Post Office funds in addition. Thus an officer graded as Deputy Assistant Director of Army Postal Services held the rank of Acting Major, but drew the pay and allowances of a Lieutenant and officers in higher appointments were similarly treated.

POSTAL SERVICES IN THEATRES OF WAR OTHER THAN FRANCE.

In Italy the Directorate of Postal Services consisted of a Deputy Director, an Assistant Director, and seven other ranks, and there was an allotment of postal personnel per Division as in France.

There were also establishments of Army Postal Services in Egypt, Salonika, N. Russia and East Africa.

Chapter VII.

DEPÔTS AND RESERVE FORMATIONS.

OWING to the great expansion of the Corps of Royal Engineers as a whole, very large increases in the establishment of the various depôts were made during the War. Short accounts of the growth of each depôt are given below.

Depôts and Reserve Units for Dismounted Men in Field Units.

Prior to mobilization it had been decided that, after the departure of the Expeditionary Force overseas, there should be one Reserve Battalion and one Depôt at Chatham. The Reserve Battalion was to consist of six companies and was to train recruits and supply reinforcements, whilst the Depôt was to consist of two companies and was to receive men returned from the Expeditionary Force and administer the establishment of the School of Military Engineering and the R.E. Band. Actually the organization of the R.E. Depôt at Chatham after mobilization remained practically the same as it had been in peace. That is to say, the Depôt consisted of :—

The Reserve Battalion (A, B, C, D, E and F Companies),
The Depôt Battalion (G, L and M Companies).

The Reserve Battalion was really the battalion, called in peace the Training Battalion, renamed. It dealt with the receiving and training of recruits. The Depôt Battalion dealt with returned Expeditionary Force men and men enlisted for special formations, such as Tunnelling Companies, Special Companies, etc.

In consequence of the appeal for the recruiting of the first 100,000 men, recruits came in at such a rate that the Reserve Battalion could not deal with the question of their accommodation. A " Billeting Battalion " was accordingly formed, to which all men that could not be dealt with by the Reserve Battalion were posted. As the demand for reinforcements and for personnel for new units increased, it was found that the Reserve Battalion could not train enough recruits. Hence the Billeting Battalion was formed into a 2nd Reserve Battalion, with a similar staff to that of the 1st Reserve Battalion, and to perform the same functions.

Similarly it was found that the Depôt Battalion could not deal with the large number of men returning from the Expeditionary Force and the inrush of recruits for special formations. To meet the situation, Provisional Companies were formed. Subsequently, to facilitate administration, these Companies and the Companies of the original Depôt Battalion were formed into two groups of Depôt Companies: No. 1 group consisted of G, L and M Depôt Companies, and one Provisional Company, and No. 2 group of four Provisional Companies.

As the formation of the New Armies proceeded, it became impossible to train at Chatham all the R.E. dismounted recruits required. Two additional Dismounted Training Centres were therefore formed— one at Newark and one at Deganwy.

There were also 2nd and 3rd Line Field Companies of the Territorial Force which trained and supplied drafts for the 1st Line Field Companies, T.F., overseas. In December, 1916, these units were grouped into five Command Groups of Reserve Field Companies, R.E., T.F. During 1917 it became apparent that this dual organization was wasteful, and as early as March, 1917, drafts of Regular and of the Territorial Force were used indiscriminately for reinforcing units overseas.

In January, 1918, the Western, Northern, Eastern and London Command Groups were abolished, and the remaining R.E. Training Centres, Reserve Battalions, and Command Groups were reconstituted into eight Reserve Battalions as follows :—

Old Unit.	New Unit.	Station.
1st Reserve Battalion	1st Reserve Battalion	Chatham.
2nd Reserve Battalion	2nd Reserve Battalion	Chattenden.
R.E. Training Centre	3rd Reserve Battalion	Newark.
R.E. Training Centre	4th Reserve Battalion	Deganwy.
Southern Command Group of Reserve Field Companies	5th Reserve Battalion	Christchurch.
Scottish Command Group of Reserve Field Companies	6th Reserve Battalion	Irvine.
Royal Monmouth R.E.S.R.	Royal Monmouth Reserve Battalion	Monmouth.
Royal Anglesey R.E.S.R.	Royal Anglesey Reserve Battalion	Beaumaris.

The establishments of all these Battalions were drawn up on similar lines. A large saving of personnel resulted, training of all recruits was carried out on the same lines and administration was facilitated. In October, 1918, the 5th Reserve Battalion at Christchurch was, as has already been mentioned, abolished to make room for a Bridging

Training Centre for two Bridging Battalions, for work with the Tank Corps.

When the above reorganization of Reserve units took place it was decided that all personnel not actually undergoing training or awaiting draft should be removed from the Reserve Battalions and posted to No. 1 Group Depôt Companies. This had the effect of making G Company of an unwieldy size, so a new Company, called Q Company, was formed to take the overflow of men from G Company. At the same time another company, called J Company, was added to No. 1 Group Depôt Companies to administer all low-medical category personnel of the Royal Engineers employed on Works Services and in Commands at home. The formation of these two companies relieved the Reserve Battalions of all purely depôt work, and left them free to carry out their proper function of training men for drafting.

Mounted Training Depôt, Aldershot.

Although this Depôt did not increase as rapidly as the Dismounted Depôt in the months following mobilization, it became necessary in 1915 to form an additional Mounted Depôt at Aldershot, larger than the one already existing, for the purpose of training the Mounted personnel required for the New Armies, and for the provision of reinforcements. The old and new Depôts were in practice administered as one large Depôt, the staffs being combined. The combined Depôt trained the whole of the mounted personnel (other than mounted personnel for Signal units) required for reinforcements and for new units (exclusive of Territorial Force units). On the reorganization of the R.E. Reserve units in January, 1918, all training of drivers for both Regular and Territorial Force reinforcements was concentrated at Aldershot.

Special Reserve Depôts.

At the outbreak of war the following Special Reserve Units existed :—

Royal Anglesey R.E.S.R. (Beaumaris) : Headquarters
1 Depôt Company.
1 Siege Company.
1 Railway Company.
Royal Monmouthshire R.E.S.R. (Monmouth): Headquarters.
1 Depôt Company.
1 Siege Company.
2 Railway Companies.

The Railway Companies proceeded to France with the original

Expeditionary Force, and eventually were absorbed into Transportation Services.

Three additional Siege Companies were raised at the Depôt of the Royal Anglesey R.E. and three additional Siege Companies and two Army Troops Companies at that of the Royal Monmouth R.E. There were thus, in all, eight R.E.S.R. Siege Companies. Two were in the Mediterranean, and subsequently became Field Companies in the 74th Division in Egypt and France. The other six were in France and were each equivalent in strength to two Army Troops Companies. The two Army Troops Companies raised at the Royal Monmouthshire Depôt also were in France.

In January, 1918, the Depôts at Beaumaris and Monmouth, as mentioned above, became Reserve Battalions for training general R.E. reinforcements.

Special Brigade Depôt.

This Depôt was formed at Withnoe, near Devonport, in June, 1916, to provide reinforcements for and deal with returned Expeditionary Force men of the Special Brigade. It was at first called " Reserve Company, Special Brigade." Originally it provided detachments for work at the Porton and Wembley Experimental Stations, which were then directly under the Ministry of Munitions. In July, 1917, however, the Porton and Wembley Establishments were made distinct R.E. units, entirely separate from the Depôt at Devonport. An increased establishment for the Special Brigade Depôt was published in January, 1918. In February, 1918, the Anti-Gas Establishment became a R.E. unit, and was considered as part of the Special Brigade.

Signal Service Depôts.

On the departure of the original Expeditionary Force overseas a Reserve Signal Company was formed at Aldershot. Owing, however, to the formation of the New Armies and the enormous growth of the Signal Service, it became necessary to move this company to stations affording greater facilities for training and accommodation, and to expand it into a Signal Service Training Centre. The headquarters of this Centre were at first at Woburn. In the neighbourhood were six Depôts which dealt with personnel in various stages of training. Later the draft-producing units of Territorial Force Divisional Signals were transferred to the Training Centre and a general pool formed from which reinforcements for Regular and Territorial Force units were supplied. The draft-producing units of the Australian, South African, and New Zealand Divisions were also transferred to the Training Centre, but they produced drafts for their own units overseas only.

In October, 1917, the H.Q. of the S.S.T.C. was moved to Bedford, and Depôts established as follows :—

Bedford A—Recruits Depôt.
Bedford B—Signalmen and Field Linesmen.
Bedford C—Operators.
Biggleswade—Air Line and Permanent Line.
Haynes Park—Riding, Driving, Saddlers, etc.
Haynes Park—Switchboard Operators.
Haynes Park—Cadet Battalion.
Hitchin—Drafts and formation of new units.

The Wireless Training Centre, which had hitherto been at Worcester, was moved to Fenny Stratford, and incorporated in the S.S.T.C. in August, 1917. In March, 1918, a new Depôt was formed at Wellingborough for training motor-cyclists. They had previously been trained at Dunstable. The Army Signal School for training officers and N.C.O.s of all arms as instructors in signalling was then formed at that place, and brought under the Signal Service Training Centre Headquarters.

Depôts Overseas.

R.E. Depôts were formed in most theatres of war. In France a General Base Depôt to administer 900 men, with permanent staff, was at first formed, and it was subsequently expanded.

Chapter VIII.

OFFICERS—ENGINEER STAFFS WITH FORMATIONS OF THE EXPEDITIONARY FORCE.

Officers, Field and L. of C. Units.

PRIOR to the War, the normal supply of Regular officers, R.E., was 30–35 annually from the R.M.A., Woolwich, and 1–3 annually from the R.M.C., Kingston, Canada. In addition, 20–25 commissions in the Special Reserve were annually given to candidates recommended as being technically qualified by the President of the Institution of Civil Engineers.

Immediately after the commencement of hostilities it was found necessary to increase the output of officers, and the length of the course at the R.M.A. was reduced to six months, whilst the further course of instruction at the S.M.E. for young officers was reduced from two years to six months.

Commissions in the Special Reserve and temporary commissions were given to candidates selected as follows :—

(1) Candidates interviewed and recommended by the President of the Institution of Civil Engineers.
(2) Candidates who were members of University O.T.C.s who possessed an engineering degree and were recommended by the O.C. of the Corps.
(3) Candidates from abroad with practical engineering experience after being interviewed by A.G.7, War Office.

The maximum limit of age was fixed at 30, though exceptions could be made in special cases.

The S.R. and T.C. officers, after being commissioned, were sent in classes of 35–40 to the S.M.E., Chatham, for a course of seven weeks' training in drill, riding, and military engineering, and were then posted straight to units ; the length of the training course was increased to 11 weeks in 1915, whilst in June, 1915, additional classes were formed at Newark in order to cope with the increased demand.

This procedure continued until the Military Service Act of 1916, when the General Staff decided that candidates for commissions should first pass through a cadet course of instruction before being commissioned.

Cadet Classes.

Cadet classes were accordingly formed at the three R.E. Centres, Chatham, Newark, and Deganwy, comprising 35 in a class; the length of the course was fixed at 11 weeks, and was subsequently extended to 16 weeks. The cadets in these classes were officers of other branches seeking transfer to the R.E. and soldiers serving for the duration of the War who had been recommended as suitable for officers—soldiers serving on pre-war attestations were not eligible for temporary commissions until May, 1918, when these commissions were opened to them. Candidates were obtained in equal proportions from Home and Expeditionary Forces, and were interviewed by a C.R.E. before being accepted for cadet classes, and interviewing by the President of the Institution of Civil Engineers was discontinued. The technical qualification required in a candidate was chiefly civil engineering, but a small proportion of electrical and mechanical engineers were accepted for the purpose of officering the units, *e.g.*, Electrical and Mechanical Companies, which required these qualifications.

Cadet Battalion.

In May, 1917, the selection of candidates for the cadet course was taken over by the General Staff, a R.E. officer being appointed G.S.O. 3 in S.D. 3 for this purpose, whilst the cadet units were concentrated at Newark into a Cadet Battalion of four Companies of 80 cadets each, and the length of the course of instruction gradually increased to six months.

Officer transfers were not admitted to the Cadet Battalion, but were formed into a separate class at Deganwy for courses of three months' instruction in engineering subjects, which were later increased to four months.

Territorial Officers.

Early in 1917, the administration of the R.E.T.F. officers, which had hitherto been carried out by the Territorial Branch at the War Office, was taken over by A.G. 7, and the commissioning of the officers, who, up to this time, were nominated by the Presidents of T.F. Associations, shortly afterwards followed the procedure for S.R. and T.C. officers.

The officers were divided into several distinct branches and were not interchangeable, each branch having its separate promotion lists as follows :—

    (i) Field Units.
    (ii) Fortress Units.
        (a) Electric Light.
        (b) Works.
    (iii) Signal Units.
    (iv) London Electrical Engineers.
    (v) Tyne Electrical Engineers.

Officers of (i) on being commissioned were sent to their Reserve Field Company Group and used as reinforcements for the Field Companies overseas; officers of (ii) to the 3rd Line units and used for the officering of the Coast Defence units; officers of (iii) to the Signal Service Training Centre for officering their Signal units at home and overseas; and officers of (iv) and (v) to the London and Tyne Electrical Engineers Depôts for officering the Coast Defence units.

On the formation of the Anti-Aircraft Searchlight Sections at home and in France the officers were drawn from the Coast Defence units and from the Depôts of the London and Tyne Electrical Engineers and, later on, the London and Tyne Electrical Engineers were made the Depôts for all Anti-Aircraft Searchlight officers and an Anti-Aircraft Searchlight School was formed at Gosport for the training of these officers.

The Reserve Field Company Groups were abolished at the end of 1917 and the officers distributed amongst the R.E. Reserve Training Centres which were formed in their place—the officers were made available to serve in any Field unit, Regular or Territorial.

Officers, Signal Service.

Amongst the Regular young officers from the R.M.A., Woolwich, the same proportion as before the War (30%) were selected for Signal Service, and after two months' training at S.M.E., Chatham, were sent to the Reserve Signal Depôt, Aldershot, for a further four months' training.

Candidates for S.R. and temporary commissions were selected as follows :—

    (1) Candidates from the University O.T.C.s who were recommended by the O.C. of the Corps and possessed a knowledge of signalling, telegraphy or electricity.
    (2) Candidates from abroad who had been employees of the big telegraph companies or in Government telegraph departments. On being commissioned they were sent to the Reserve Signal Depôt, Aldershot, for a course of seven weeks before being posted to their units.

In 1915, when the Reserve Signal Depôt at Aldershot was broken up, and the Signal Service Training Centre at Bedford was formed, the classes for officers were continued at the latter place, and the length of the course for S.R. and T.C. officers extended to 12 weeks, and later, when the Cadet units were introduced, alternate classes of cadets and officers of other branches of the service were formed and the length of the courses extended finally to six months.

Officers, Tunnelling Companies.

Early in 1915 it was found necessary to raise specialized Tunnelling Companies for the mining operations in France, and, in order to obtain the most suitable material for the officering of these Companies, all the mining institutions in Great Britain were circularized for recommendations, whilst candidates from abroad with mining experience who had been employed in responsible positions were specially earmarked for temporary commissions in these companies. A special office, designated the "Tunnelling Depôt," was formed in London, where all candidates for commissions were examined regarding their technical qualifications before being sent to A.G. 7, War Office, for final interview. At first the service was so urgent that it was only possible to give the officers about a week's military instruction at Chatham before sending them to France, where technical knowledge was the principal requirement, but when the immediate urgency was over, officers were sent for a 12 days' course in Mine Rescue work at Dudley before being sent to Chatham for a fortnight's course of military instruction, whilst later the Mine Rescue classes were transferred to Chatham and the total course lengthened to five weeks. Finally, the "Tunnelling Depôt" was abolished and candidates were sent as cadets to the R.E. Cadet Battalion at Newark for a three months' course before being selected for the Mining and Mine Rescue course at Chatham.

Officers, Other Specialist Units.

The officers of other specialized services, such as Special Brigade, Field Survey Battalion, Camouflage Park, Meteorological Section, Forestry Directorate, Carrier Pigeon Service, etc., were obtained either by transfer of officers from other branches of the service possessing the special technical qualifications required, or by commissioning suitably qualified civilians and sending them to France, where they were instructed in the duties of their particular branch and in such military details as were considered necessary. Depôts were afterwards formed for the Special Brigade, Survey Battalions and Meteorological Sections respectively, where additional instruction was given to officers before proceeding overseas, and, when the cadet organization was introduced, candidates were sent for a cadet course with an Infantry Officer Cadet Battalion before being commissioned and joining their respective Depôts.

FIELD ENGINEERS.

In the early days of the War, these officers were required on the staff of the C.E.s of Armies and Corps overseas for special duties in connection with hutments, roads, water supply, camps, etc., and were selected by A.G. 7 from Civil Engineers of high technical ability up to the age of 45. They were given temporary commissions as Lieutenants or Captains, R.E., and sent overseas without any military training.

OFFICERS OF THE LABOUR BATTALIONS, R.E.

Eleven of these battalions were raised from men of the navvy class, and the officers were selected from civil engineers and contractors by F.W. Branch. No age limit was fixed, and they were given direct commissions as Lieutenants and Captains, R.E., and sent to the assembly place of the battalions at Southampton, whence they proceeded overseas as the battalions were completed. These battalions were later transferred to the General Labour Corps.

ROYAL ANGLESEY AND ROYAL MONMOUTHSHIRE ROYAL ENGINEERS. (SPECIAL RESERVE).

These were the only Special Reserve R.E. units in existence before the War, and they were expanded during the War from four to ten companies. The extra officers required were at first nominated by the O.C.s of the units, given direct commissions in the Special Reserve, and trained at the Depôts at Beaumaris and Monmouth, but when the cadet organization was introduced, candidates were selected and trained in the same way as other S.R. and T.C. officers, and earmarked for these units at the request of the C.O.s.

COMBING OUT.

In the middle of 1917, arrangements were made to replace, as far as possible, all fit officers of the R.E. Units of the Home Service Divisions and Mixed Brigades (at home) by unfit officers from the Reserve Training Centres, so as to make the former available for drafting overseas. Early in 1918, a comb out of the officers of the Fortress units on Home Defence who were fit for General Service and under the age of 36 was made ; and these officers were sent to Deganwy for a four months' course of instruction, before being made available for drafting overseas, and were replaced by wounded and unfit officers from the Reserve Training Centres. The officers employed on Engineer Services at home were treated in the same way, but it was not found possible to extend the same policy to officers of the Anti-Aircraft units in England, as there were no wounded or unfit officers with the necessary qualifications and training to replace them.

RELEASES.

A large number of R.E. officers were applied for by the Ministry of Munitions throughout the War for work in the Ministry itself or with controlled firms. The policy was to allow officers to go, if unfit, until they became fit for general service; but it was found a matter of difficulty to induce the Ministry or controlled firms to release them when they became fit.

EXCHANGES.

Towards the end of 1917, a system was inaugurated of bringing home from Expeditionary Forces senior officers who were suffering from the strain of active service, and either posting them to home appointments for the duration of the War, or retaining them for a tour of six months before again sending them overseas. In the former case they replaced retired officers who were relegated to the Retired List. Early in 1918, the system of six months' home service tours was extended to officers of all ranks of the Field and Signal Service Units, and exchanges effected on completion of the tour.

DRAFTING.

In order to replace casualties in the Field, " pools " of officers were formed at the bases of Expeditionary Forces, and these pools were maintained by demands in bulk on the War Office. The demands were met from the different Reserve Training Centres and Depôts according to the number of officers available at each. The Reserve Training Centres were maintained by posting newly commissioned Temporary and Territorial officers and officers invalided from Expeditionary Forces on becoming fit for duty again. Exclusive of new formations, the following are approximately the numbers of officers sent overseas in response to demands from Expeditionary Forces :—

	1914.	1915.	1916.	1917.	1918.	Total.
Field Units	23	181	438	862	940	2444
Signal Units	22	124	303	401	584	1434
Tunnelling Units	—	141	351	202	91	785
Special Brigade Units	—	13	21	70	89	193
Miscellaneous	38	239	34	209	93	613
	83	698	1147	1744	1797	5469

ENGINEER STAFFS WITH FORMATIONS OF THE EXPEDITIONARY FORCES.

The 1914 *War Establishments* and *Field Service Regulations* contained little on the subject of R.E. organization ; in fact, the word " Engineers " did not appear at all in the index of *F.S. Regulations, Pt. II.* The original Expeditionary Force was accompanied by one Brigadier-General, R.E., with G.H.Q., and a Colonel, R.E., with the Headquarters at each of the two Corps. These officers were charged with the duty of giving " technical advice on Engineer matters," but they had no administrative powers or executive authority of any kind, and in each case their staff consisted of one clerk only. The Engineer units in each Division were commanded by a C.R.E., whose duties and staff remained substantially unchanged throughout the War, and, despite various proposals and recommendations, until the present day.

The only Engineer officer to whom the powers of a Director were given was the Director of Works, whose duties were confined to the Lines of Communication and Bases. The story of the development of this Directorate is told fully in the volume entitled " Work under the Director of Works—France," and will not be referred to again here.

It will be clear that there was, thus, a large gap in Engineer control in the field, since no authority existed between C.R.E.s of Divisions and the Director of Works on L. of C. Practically this state of affairs was changed almost at once, for the B.G.R.E. and Unit Engineers perforce assumed executive duties and financial responsibility, which were not officially given to them till a much later date. The rapid growth and expansion of the Army is described in other parts of this book, but for the utilization, control and superintendence of the vastly increased Engineer personnel and material, no organization had been provided.

When the 1st and 2nd Armies were formed at the beginning of 1915, the establishment did not at first provide for even a Royal Engineer technical adviser; the two Corps Commanders who were promoted to command the Armies carried off with them their Engineer staffs, and eventually official sanction was given for Army Engineer staffs.

In January, 1915, the title of B.G.R.E. at G.H.Q. was changed to " Chief Engineer Expeditionary Force," and the Colonels, R.E., attached to Corps Headquarters, were also given the title of Chief Engineer. A little later all these officers were formally granted the powers of a Director of Works. In April of the same year the Chief Engineer at G.H.Q. was renamed Engineer-in-Chief, with the rank of Major-General, and Chief Engineers of Corps and Armies became Brigadier-Generals. At a later date Army Chief Engineers were given the rank of Major-General, and these were the grades that existed at the end of the War. It would scarcely be possible or profitable to trace in detail the development of the staff of the Engineer-in-Chief and Chief-Engineers, but some of the principal features will be mentioned shortly. At G.H.Q. the first pressing need was to collect Engineer information, which was almost entirely lacking, and to produce an organization for dealing with the repair of roads and bridges in an advance.[1] Very soon, too, a vast amount of administrative work had to be done in connection with the provision and distribution of new units and Engineer personnel, and by the middle of 1915 the staff of the E.-in-C. had grown from one clerk to four officers and 15 clerks and draughtsmen ; by the end of the War these numbers were multiplied by five.

Special technical officers were continually called for ; thus, early in 1915, a qualified Bridge Engineer was brought in ; in June, 1915, a Geological Adviser, especially for water supply, was obtained through the Director of the Geological Survey of England, and in 1916 a second geologist was added for work in connection with mining. Mining operations assumed such importance that a special staff, headed by an Inspector, grew up under the Engineer-in-Chief, and by 1916 this alone amounted to six officers and eight clerks and draughtsmen. In 1918 a special Inspector of R.E. Machinery, who also acted as Water Supply Adviser to the E.-in-C., was appointed to co-ordinate the work of the Army Electrical and Mechanical Companies.[2]

Also in the summer of 1918 an additional Assistant Engineer-in-Chief (Lieut.-Colonel) was appointed to organize and control the work of the special concrete units[3] whose work was expected to assume great importance during the coming winter. (*See* section of this volume headed " Concrete Defences and Factories.")

New Establishments were approved not very long before the Armistice, a copy of which is given below :—

GENERAL HEADQUARTERS, 1ST ECHELON.
ATTACHED TO G.H.Q.
R.E.

Engineer-in-Chief	1
Deputy Engineers-in-Chief (*a*)	2
Assistants to Engineer-in-Chief (*b*)	4
Staff Officers to Engineer-in-Chief (*c*)	2
Clerks	31
Batmen	11
Drivers, A.S.C., M.T.	7

[1] *See* volume entitled " Bridging."
[2] *See* volume entitled " Water Supply—France."
[3] These Companies were lent by the D.G. Transportation, and are not, therefore, referred to in the general account of the development of the Corps.

Mines.

Assistant Inspector (*b*)	1
Assistant Inspector (Captain)	1
Mechanical Engineer (Major or Captain)	1
Geologist (Major or Captain)	1
Medical Officer (Mine Rescue expert)	1
Clerks	8
Batmen	3
Drivers, A.S.C., M.T.	2
Attached Officers (*d*)	5
Batmen	3
Driver, A.S.C., M.T.	1

(*a*) Brigadier-Generals—one to be Inspector of Mines.
(*b*) Lieutenant-Colonels (Class X).
(*c*) 1 Class BB., 1 Class FF.
(*d*) 1 Lieutenant-Colonel, 4 Majors or Captains R.E.

As regards Chief Engineers, a long time elapsed before any fixed establishment was approved. Early in 1915 three Field Engineers were attached to each Corps Chief Engineer, one of whom acted as staff officer, while the other two dealt with roads, bridges and water supply behind Divisional areas. Later a fourth was added in some cases to take charge of hutting. A clerk and draughtsman were also provided during this year.

In 1916 the extensive preparations for the Battle of the Somme necessitated special staffs being formed under the Chief Engineers of the Third and Fourth Armies for water supply and roads. Important changes took place in 1917 in two respects. The formation of the Transportation Directorate relieved Chief Engineers of responsibility for road maintenance. At the same time the formation of Army Electrical and Mechanical Companies and Workshop Companies, and also of additional Army Troops Companies for hutting and other constructional services, threw an increasing amount of administrative work on Chief Engineers, and this led to the appointment in both Armies and Corps of a C.R.E., Army (or Corps) Troops, with an Adjutant and small clerical staff. About the same time the staff officers to Chief Engineers were given formal staff gradings, the S.O.R.E., Army, being graded as a D.A.A.G., and S.O.R.E., Corps, as a Brigade-Major. These were subsequently altered to the grades shown in the Establishments below, which are those that existed at the time of the Armistice :—

HEADQUARTERS OF AN ARMY.

ATTACHED TO HEADQUARTERS OF AN ARMY.

Chief Engineer	1
Staff Officer to Chief Engineer (Class B.B.)	1

Field Engineers (a)	4
Clerks	5
Commanding Royal Engineer (Lieut.-Colonel)	1
Adjutant (Captain or Subaltern)	1
Clerks and Draughtsmen	2
Controller of Mines	1
Assistant Controller of Mines	1
Clerks	2

(a) 2 Majors, 2 Captains.

Headquarters of a Corps.

Attached to Headquarters of a Corps.

Chief Engineer (Brigadier-General) (b)	1
Staff Officer to Chief Engineer (Class F.F.)	1
Field Engineers (c)	3
Engineer Clerks	3
Draughtsman	1
Commanding Royal Engineer (Lieut.-Colonel)	1
Adjutant (Captain or Subaltern)	1
Clerks and Draughtsmen	2

(b) Acts as technical adviser in Engineer matters.
(c) 1 Major, 1 Captain, 1 Lieutenant.

CHAPTER IX.

ADMINISTRATION.

OFFICE OF A.A.G., R.E.

THE branch of the War Office designated A.G. 7 came into existence in the year 1846 to administer the personnel of the Corps of Royal Engineers. Up till 1904 the A.A.G., R.E., acted directly under the Adjutant-General. From that year the branch came under the Director of Personal Services and the Director of Recruiting and Organization, and so continued up to and during the War.

At the outbreak of the War the branch consisted of the A.A.G., a superintending officer, and nine clerks. On mobilization it was immediately increased by one Staff Captain and six clerks, and by the end of the War had expanded to a total establishment of nine officers and 37 clerks. Up till May, 1917, the work of the branch was not definitely subdivided. The most important work during the period was the formation of new units. It was necessary for the A.A.G., R.E., to keep in the very closest touch with the O. i/c R.E. Records. The latter, therefore, visited the former at least once a week to discuss outstanding questions. This worked fairly well, but all statistical and other information about " other ranks " which was required had to be obtained from the Record Office, and this caused difficulties and delays. The branch was therefore reorganized into two sub-branches as follows :—A D.A.A.G. [A.G. 7 (a)] was appointed to deal with all work concerning officers, and an officer was brought from the Record Office and appointed D.A.A.G. [A.G. 7 (b)] to deal with all " other ranks " work. This latter sub-branch developed a statistical bureau of its own, so that information required in considering man-power requirements, combing out, drafting, etc., should be more readily available.

RECORD OFFICES.

The original R.E. Record Office which existed prior to the War was largely augmented as the War proceeded, and when the formation of the New Armies commenced in August, 1914, a second Record Office was established, also at Chatham, to deal with them. In May, 1915, the two Record Offices were amalgamated into one, which dealt with all R.E., except the R.E. (T.F.), till February, 1917, when it took over the record work of the Territorial R.E. also. In January, 1918, a separate Record Office to deal with the personnel of the R.E.

(Transportation) was formed in London, and relieved the main R.E. Record Office of all work in this connection. Base Record Offices were formed during the War in France, Egypt and Salonika, their establishments depending on the number of Divisions in each theatre of war.

Drafting.

During the latter part of 1917, the preparation and ordering of drafts (other ranks) was taken over by the A.G.7 (*b*) sub-branch from the O. i/c Records. Demands for officer reinforcements were dealt with by the A.G.7 (*a*) sub-branch, where it was decided from which Reserve Training Centre the officer reinforcements were to be sent.

Combing Out.

Combing out of officers is dealt with in the Chapter relating to officers. As regards other ranks, it became necessary early in 1917 to comb out A category men from units at home and send them overseas. At this time the R.E. units at home were nearly all Territorial units full of A category men, who had enlisted on Territorial engagements for home service only, but who had become liable for service overseas on the passing of the Military Service Acts. Low category men were enlisted or transferred from other arms and, when trained, were used to replace the A category men referred to above. Towards the end of 1917 combing out was extended to B1 category men.

Most of the men combed out were utilized as reinforcements for R.E. overseas. Some, however, were transferred to other Corps. Thus 5,000 men were transferred to the Infantry in November, 1916, 8,000 to Pioneer Battalions in July and August, 1917, and 2,000 to the Tank Corps early in 1918.

Supply of Tradesmen.

During the first two years of the War no difficulty was experienced in getting tradesmen in sufficient numbers. This was because under the voluntary system tradesmen preferred to enlist in the R.E., and men could be spared from civil workshops. From the beginning of 1917, however, the supply fell off owing to the protection of most classes of tradesmen in Munition and other works, and to the fact that tradesmen in Category A who came up for service were posted to Infantry unless they were in a trade (e.g., electrician) to the members of which a pledge had been given that when called up they would be employed in a technical Corps. The shortage was most felt in blacksmiths, and other important trades which were also short were carpenters, bricklayers and plumbers. Men of other trades, and pioneers, were sent overseas in lieu of men of the trades in which there was a shortage, and the War did not last long enough for any serious inconvenience to be caused by this dilution.

RELEASES.

During the War a very large number of men were released from the R.E. to work in a civil capacity. Men were released for munition work, agriculture, ship building, mining, and many other functions. Only a small percentage of these men ever returned to the Colours. The R.E. being composed mainly of tradesmen, a larger number in proportion to the total strength was taken from the R.E. than from other arms. The total number of men released from the R.E. to various classes of the Army Reserve in this way was approximately 7,900. This figure does not include large numbers lent to various departments and granted leave for the purpose, nor 10,000 attested Post Office men, nor men released for agricultural furlough by O.C.s units, nor men released for indefinite periods for duty with the Labour Corps.

PROMOTION (OTHER RANKS).

During the War the R.E. Corps Promotion Roster for Old Army N.C.O.s was not expanded. All Old Army warrant officers, N.C.O.s and men only received *substantive* promotion as vacancies occurred on the Corps Roster.

New Army and Territorial N.C.O.s received substantive promotion within the establishments of units in which they were serving, provided the vacancies they filled were caused by certain casualties of a more or less permanent nature. This applied to units in the theatres of war only.

Old Army N.C.O.s filling vacancies as above were, under instructions issued in 1917, given acting rank, which they were allowed to retain for six months after relinquishing their appointment through sickness, wounds, etc. In September, 1918, such N.C.O.s were given temporary instead of acting rank, and the six months' limit for retention of rank was abolished.

Promotion at home was "acting" only, except promotion of Old Army N.C.O.s on the original Corps Roster. On proceeding overseas the acting rank was relinquished, unless the N.C.O. went overseas with a unit or in exchange for an N.C.O. serving overseas. In 1918, however, instructions were issued allowing N.C.O.s drafted overseas to retain their acting rank for one month after disembarkation. If they were not absorbed in their rank in a unit in that time they were required to revert to their substantive rank.

The promotion of N.C.O.s serving overseas but not with an Expeditionary Force was "acting" only till June, 1918, when it was brought into line with promotion of N.C.O.s in theatres of war. No substantive promotion to Warrant Officers, Class I., was given except to Old Army W.O.s, Class II., to fill vacancies on the Corps Roster. All other vacancies were filled by promotion to the temporary rank of W.O. Class I.

GROWTH OF THE ROYAL ENGINEERS.
(a) Regulars and Special Reserve.

	1st August, 1914.			1st August, 1915.					1st August, 1916.					1st August, 1917.			Serving in				
Total strength:—																					
Officers	1,056			3,049					6,823					8,886							
Other ranks	10,394			82,932					154,361					230,500							
Description of Units.	Number of Units.	Serving at Home.	Serving in Colonies.	Number of Units.	Serving at Home.	Serving in Colonies.	B.E.F.	M.E.F.	Number of Units.	Serving at Home.	Serving in Colonies.	B.E.F.	M.E.F., etc.	Number of Units.	Serving at Home.	Serving in Colonies.	France.	Egypt.	Salonika.	East Africa.	Mesopotamia.
Depôts	3	3	—	7	5	—	1	1	15	13	—	1	1	19	15	—	1	1	1	—	1
Field Companies	15	13	2	103	12	—	77	14	109	—	—	95	14	113	1	—	98	—	11	—	3
Fortress Companies	31	16	15	49	34	9	6	—	21	12	9	36	9	20	11	—	40	3	7	—	—
Army Troops Companies	—	—	—	—	—	—	—	—	47	2	—	—	—	50	—	—	—	—	—	—	—
Engineer Field Park (late 47th Base Park Company)	—	—	2	—	—	—	—	—	—	—	—	—	—	1	—	—	—	—	—	—	—
Signal Units	17	15	—	110	5	—	74	31	268	11	—	187	70	321	3	—	228	37	30	11	12
Signal Depôts	—	—	—	8	6	—	1	1	9	7	—	1	1	11	6	—	1	1	1	1	1
Railway Operating Divisions	—	—	—	—	—	—	—	—	25	6	—	18	1	4	1	—	1	1	1	—	—
Railway Units	2	2	—	3	—	—	3	—	25	—	—	17	8	122	—	—	105	6	11	—	—
Railway Companies (Special Res.)	3	3	—	3	—	—	3	—	3	—	—	3	—	3	—	—	—	2	—	—	—
Field Troops	1	1	—	—	—	—	—	—	4	—	—	3	—	3	—	—	3	—	—	—	—
Field Squadrons	1	1	—	3	—	—	3	—	3	—	—	3	—	5	—	—	5	—	—	—	—
Bridging Trains	2	2	—	3	1	—	2	—	—	—	—	—	—	—	—	—	—	—	—	—	—
Pontoon Park Companies	—	—	—	—	—	—	—	—	12	2	—	10	3	12	—	—	12	—	—	—	—
Base Park Companies	—	—	—	1	—	—	1	1	5	—	—	2	2	5	—	—	3	—	1	1	—
Advanced Park Companies	—	—	—	1	—	—	1	—	4	—	—	5	—	3	—	—	3	—	1	—	—
Tunnelling Companies	—	—	—	9	—	—	9	—	25	—	—	25	—	25	—	—	25	—	—	—	—
Special Companies	—	—	—	5	—	—	5	—	5*	—	—	5*	—	29	—	—	29	—	—	—	—
Quarrying Companies	—	—	—	—	—	—	—	—	2	—	—	2	—	10	—	—	10	—	—	—	—
Land Drainage Companies	—	—	—	—	—	—	—	—	2	—	—	2	—	—	—	—	—	—	—	—	—
Survey Companies	3	3	—	2	2	—	—	—	5	5	—	1	—	7	1	—	5	1	1	—	—
Printing Companies	1	1	—	1	—	—	1	—	1	—	—	1	—	1	1	—	—	1	1	—	—
Printing Sections	—	—	—	2	—	—	2	—	6	1	—	4	2	3	—	—	1	1	1	—	—
Special Works Companies	—	—	—	1	—	—	1	—	1	—	—	1	—	1	—	—	1	—	1	1	—

* The Special Brigade was divided into Battalions, Companies and Sections.

GROWTH OF THE ROYAL ENGINEERS—continued.
(a) REGULARS AND SPECIAL RESERVE—continued.

Description of Units.	1st August, 1914.			1st August, 1915.					1st August, 1916.					1st August, 1917.							
																	Serving in				
	Number of Units.	Serving at Home.	Serving in Colonies.	Number of Units.	Serving at Home.	Serving in Colonies.	B.E.F.	M.E.F.	Number of Units.	Serving at Home.	Serving in Colonies.	B.E.F.	M.E.F., etc.	Number of Units.	Serving at Home.	Serving in Colonies.	France.	Egypt.	Salonika.	East Africa.	Mesopotamia.
Field Companies (Special Res.)	2	—	—	2	—	—	—	2	2	—	—	—	2	2	—	—	6	2	—	—	—
Siege Companies (Special Res.)	1	2	—	6	—	—	6	—	6	—	—	6	—	6	—	—	6	1	1	—	—
Postal Section	—	1	—	2†	1	—	1	—	2†	1	—	1	—	4	1	—	4	1	—	—	—
Anti-Aircraft Searchlight Cos.	—	—	—	2	—	—	2	—	2	—	—	2	—	4	—	—	4	—	—	—	—
Ranging Sections	1	—	—	2	2	—	2	—	1	2	—	1	—	2	2	—	1	—	—	—	—
R. Anglesey R.E. Depôts (Special Reserve)	—	1	—	—	—	—	—	—	—	—	—	—	—	—	—	—	—	—	—	—	—
Wagon Erecting Companies	1	—	—	2	2	—	—	—	2	2	—	—	—	2	2	—	—	—	—	—	—
R. Monmouth R.E. Depôt (Special Reserve)	—	—	—	—	—	—	—	—	—	—	—	—	—	4	—	—	4	—	—	—	—
Inland Water Transport Depôt and Stores	—	—	—	2	1	—	—	—	2	2	—	—	—	2	2	—	—	—	—	—	—
Inland Water Transport Sections	—	—	—	—	—	—	1	—	24	10	1	11	3	23	6	1	14	1	1	1	1
Topographical Sections	—	—	—	—	—	—	—	—	2	—	—	—	1	1	—	—	1	—	—	—	—
Carrier Pigeon Service	—	—	—	—	—	—	—	—	3	—	—	1	2	3	—	—	1	1	1	—	—
Meteorological Sections	—	—	—	—	—	—	—	—	3	—	—	1	2	2	—	—	1	—	1	—	—
Artisan Works Companies	—	—	—	—	—	—	—	—	2	—	—	2	—	7	—	—	7	—	—	—	—
Electrical and Mechanical Co.	—	—	—	—	—	—	—	—	—	—	—	—	—	9	1	—	8	—	—	—	—
Engineer Services	1	1	—	1†	1	—	—	—	1†	1	—	1	—	1†	1	—	—	—	—	—	—
Coast Works Companies	—	—	—	—	—	—	—	—	—	—	—	—	—	2	2	—	—	—	—	—	—
Road Construction Companies	—	—	—	—	—	—	—	—	—	—	—	—	—	2	—	—	—	—	—	—	—
Army Troops Companies (Special Reserve)	—	—	—	—	—	—	—	—	—	—	—	—	—	33	—	—	33	—	—	—	—
Cavalry Corps Bridging Park	—	—	—	—	—	—	—	—	—	—	—	—	—	2	—	—	2	—	—	—	—
Forestry Companies	—	—	—	—	—	—	—	—	—	—	—	—	—	1	—	—	1	—	—	—	—
Water Boring Sections	—	—	—	—	—	—	—	—	—	—	—	—	—	5	—	—	5	—	—	—	—
Total	85	66	19	332	72†	9	202	49	652	72	10	445	125	891	54	9	663	60	70	14	21

† The establishment of units was considerably increased to provide for Postal Services and Engineer Services in all theatres of operations.

GROWTH OF THE ROYAL ENGINEERS—continued.

(b) TERRITORIAL FORCE.

Total strength:—																
Officers	513			1,262								} 56,282				
Other ranks	13,127			38,924												

Description of Units.	1st August, 1914.			1st August, 1915.					1st August, 1916.					1st August, 1917.							
																	Serving in				
	Number of Units.	Serving at Home.	Serving in Colonies.	Number of Units.	Serving at Home.	Serving in Colonies.	B.E.F.	M.E.F.	Number of Units.	Serving at Home.	Serving in Colonies.	B.E.F.	M.E.F., etc.	Number of Units.	Serving at Home.	Serving in Colonies.	France.	Egypt.	Salonika.	East Africa.	Mesopotamia.
Reserve Field Companies	—	—	—	—	—	—	—	—	—	—	—	—	—	15	15	—	—	—	—	—	—
Field Companies	28	28	—	—	—	—	—	—	—	—	—	—	—	110	31	—	58	13	5	—	3
Army Troops Companies	15	15	—	—	—	—	—	—	—	—	—	—	—	14	—	—	12	2	—	—	—
Signal Units	14	14	—	—	—	—	—	—	—	—	—	—	—	36	12	—	16	6	2	—	—
Anti-Aircraft Companies	—	—	—	—	—	—	—	—	—	—	—	—	—	35	35	—	—	—	—	—	—
Anti-Aircraft Sections	18	18	—	—	—	—	—	—	—	—	—	—	—	42	—	—	42	—	—	—	—
Electric Light Companies	24	24	—	—	—	—	—	—	—	—	—	—	—	44	43	1	—	—	—	—	—
Searchlight Companies	1	1	—	—	—	—	—	—	—	—	—	—	—	3	3	—	—	—	—	—	—
Works Companies	—	—	—	—	—	—	—	—	—	—	—	—	—	15	14	1	—	—	—	—	—
Postal Service	—	—	—	—	—	—	—	—	—	—	—	—	—	1	1	—	—	—	—	—	—
Aeroplane Squadrons, Searchlight Sections	—	—	—	—	—	—	—	—	—	—	—	—	—	3	3	—	—	—	—	—	—
Demolition Sections	—	—	—	—	—	—	—	—	—	—	—	—	—	2	2	—	—	—	—	—	—
Nos. 1 and 3 Cos., Tyne E.E.	4	4	—	—	—	—	—	—	—	—	—	—	—	2	2	—	—	—	—	—	—
Nos. 1–5 Cos., London E.E.	6	6	—	—	—	—	—	—	—	—	—	—	—	5	5	—	—	—	—	—	—
Depôts	—	—	—	—	—	—	—	—	—	—	—	—	—	3	3	—	—	—	—	—	—
Total	110	110	—	—	—	—	—	—	—	—	—	—	—	330	169	2	128	21	7	—	3

GROWTH OF THE ROYAL ENGINEERS—continued.

(c) REGULARS, SPECIAL RESERVE AND TERRITORIAL FORCE (EXCLUSIVE OF THE ROYAL ENGINEERS, TRANSPORTATION BRANCH).

1st August, 1918.

Total strength :—
  Officers 11,830
  Other ranks 225,540

Description of Units.	Number of Units.	Serving at Home.	Serving in Colonies.	Serving in France.	Egypt.	Salonika.	Mesopotamia.	East Africa.	Italy.
Depôts	24	15	—	6	1	1	1	—	—
Field Companies	231	40	—	155	12	13	6	—	5
Field Company (R.M.R.E.)	1	—	—	—	1	—	—	—	—
Field Company (R.A.R.E.)	1	—	—	1	—	—	—	—	—
Field Squadrons	6	—	—	5	1	—	—	—	—
Field Troops	3	—	—	—	2	—	1	—	—
Army Troops	67	—	—	52	7	7	—	—	1
Army Troops (R.M.R.E.)	2	—	—	2	—	—	—	—	—
Siege Companies (R.M.R.E.)	3	—	—	3	—	—	—	—	—
Siege Companies (R.A.R.E.)	3	—	—	3	—	—	—	—	—
Inspector of Searchlights	1	—	—	1	—	—	—	—	—
Field Searchlight Companies	2	—	—	1	—	—	—	1	—
Overseas Branch Ordnance Survey Company	1	—	—	1	—	—	—	—	—
Survey Companies	9	1	—	6	1	1	—	—	—
Topographical Section	1	—	—	—	—	—	—	1	—
Printing Companies	2	—	—	2	—	—	—	—	—
Printing Sections	4	—	—	2	1	—	—	1	—
Bridging and Engineer Field Parks	2	—	—	1	—	—	1	—	—
Bridging School	1	—	—	1	—	—	—	—	—
Advanced Park Companies	3	—	—	1	1	1	—	—	—
Base Park Companies	8	—	—	4	2	1	—	1	—
Pontoon Park Companies	13	—	—	11	1	—	—	—	1
Electrical and Mechanical Cos.	9	—	—	7	—	—	2	—	—
Water Boring Companies	5	—	—	5	—	—	—	—	—
Water Supply Companies	3	—	—	—	3	—	—	—	—
Sound Ranging Sections	2	—	—	—	2	—	—	—	—
Reserve Battalions (35 Companies)	6	6	—	—	—	—	—	—	—
Reserve Battalion (R.M.R.E.) (3 Companies)	1	1	—	—	—	—	—	—	—
Reserve Battalion (R.A.R.E.) (3 Companies)	1	1	—	—	—	—	—	—	—
Group Depôt Companies (11 Cos.)	2	2	—	—	—	—	—	—	—
Foreway Companies	10	—	—	10	—	—	—	—	—
Tunnelling Companies	25	—	—	25	—	—	—	—	—
H.Q. Special Brigade (Chemists)	1	—	—	1	—	—	—	—	—
Battalions Special Brigade (16 Companies) (Chemists)	4	—	—	4	—	—	—	—	—
"Z" Special Company (Chemists)	1	—	—	1	—	—	—	—	—
H.Q. Special Companies (Chemists)	4	—	—	4	—	—	—	—	—
Special Factory Section (Chemists)	1	—	—	1	—	—	—	—	—
Special Store (Chemists)	1	—	—	1	—	—	—	—	—
Anti-Gas Service (Chemists)	1	—	—	1	—	—	—	—	—
Gas Directorate (Chemists)	1	—	—	1	—	—	—	—	—
Meteorological Sections	4	1	—	1	1	1	—	—	—
Special Works Park	2	1	—	1	—	—	—	—	—
Land Drainage Company	1	—	—	1	—	—	—	—	—
Artisan Works Companies	16	—	—	16	—	—	—	—	—
Establishment of Controller of Mines	1	—	—	1	—	—	—	—	—
Army Mine Schools	4	—	—	4	—	—	—	—	—

GROWTH OF THE ROYAL ENGINEERS—*Continued*.

(c) REGULARS, SPECIAL RESERVE AND TERRITORIAL FORCE (EXCLUSIVE OF THE ROYAL ENGINEERS, TRANSPORTATION BRANCH).

Description of Units.	Number of Units.	Serving at Home.	Serving in Colonies.	Serving in France.	Egypt.	Salonika.	Mesopotamia.	East Africa.	Italy.
Forestry Control for Army Areas	1	—	—	1	—	—	—	—	—
L. of C. Forestry Group	1	—	—	1	—	—	—	—	—
Directorate of Forestry	1	—	—	1	—	—	—	—	—
L. of C. Forests	1	—	—	1	—	—	—	—	—
Forestry Companies	11	—	—	11	—	—	—	—	—
Anti-Aircraft Searchlight Cos.	17	17	—	—	—	—	—	—	—
Anti-Aircraft Searchlight Sections	70	—	—	70	—	—	—	—	—
R.E. Workshops	5	—	—	5	—	—	—	—	—
Electric Light Section	1	—	—	1	—	—	—	—	—
Base Army Anti-Gas School	1	—	—	—	—	1	—	—	—
Divisional Army Anti-Gas Schools	4	—	—	—	—	4	—	—	—
G.H.Q., 3rd Echelon	4	—	—	1	1	1	1	—	—
General Headquarters	1	—	—	—	1	—	—	—	—
H.Q. R.E., Hockwold	1	1	—	—	—	—	—	—	—
Divisional H.Q. Engineers	60	5	—	41	7	4	2	—	1
H.Q. Guards Divisional Engineers	1	—	—	1	—	—	—	—	—
Postal Sections	6	1	—	1	1	1	—	1	1
Entrenching Battalion	1	—	—	1	—	—	—	—	—
17th Corps Laundry	1	—	—	1	—	—	—	—	—
Indian Expeditionary Force	1	—	—	1	—	—	—	—	—
G.H.Q. Kennels	1	—	—	1	—	—	—	—	—
Fortress Companies	37	27	10	—	—	—	—	—	—
Fortress Works Companies	5	5	—	—	—	—	—	—	—
Works Companies	17	11	1	4	—	—	1	—	—
"H" Company (K.G.O. Sappers and Miners)	1	—	—	—	—	—	1	—	—
Cinema Company	1	—	—	—	—	—	1	—	—
Emergency Sections	2	2	—	—	—	—	—	—	—
Tyne Electrical Engineers	1	1	—	—	—	—	—	—	—
London Electrical Engineers	1	1	—	—	—	—	—	—	—
R.E. Cadet Battalion	1	1	—	—	—	—	—	—	—
Experimental Company (Esher)	1	1	—	—	—	—	—	—	—
Motor Cyclists (Command and Home Defences)	1	1	—	—	—	—	—	—	—
H.Q. Staffs Group Reserve Field Company	1	1	—	—	—	—	—	—	—
School of Electric Light (Stokes Bay)	1	1	—	—	—	—	—	—	—
R.E. Section (Yatesbury)	1	1	—	—	—	—	—	—	—
R.M. College (Camberley)	1	1	—	—	—	—	—	—	—
R.M. Academy (Woolwich)	1	1	—	—	—	—	—	—	—
Base Signal Depôts	6	—	—	2	1	1	1	1	—
Signal Service Training Centre	1	1	—	—	—	—	—	—	—
Divisional Signal Companies	70	5	—	52	5	4	2	—	2
Cyclists Divisional Signal Company	1	1	—	—	—	—	—	—	—
G.H.Q. Signal Companies	5	1	—	1	1	1	—	—	1
Army H.Q. Signal Companies	4	—	—	4	—	—	—	—	—
Reserve H.Q. Signal Company	1	—	—	1	—	—	—	—	—
Army Corps Signal Companies	24	1	—	16	3	2	1	—	1
Indian Army Corps Signal Cos.	3	—	—	—	—	—	3	—	—
Army Signal Schools	7	—	—	5	—	1	1	—	—
Corps Signal School	1	—	—	1	—	—	—	—	—
Cavalry Corps Signal Squadron	1	—	—	1	—	—	—	—	—
Cavalry Divisional Signal Squadrons	5	—	—	4	1	—	—	—	—
Signal Construction Companies	5	—	—	5	—	—	—	—	—
Reserve Signal Troops	2	2	—	—	—	—	—	—	—
Signal Troops	8	—	—	8	—	—	—	—	—
Light Railway Signal Sections	6	—	—	5	1	—	—	—	—

E

GROWTH OF THE ROYAL ENGINEERS—Continued.

(c) REGULARS, SPECIAL RESERVE AND TERRITORIAL FORCE (EXCLUSIVE OF THE ROYAL ENGINEERS, TRANSPORTATION BRANCH).

Description of Units.	Number of Units.	Serving at Home.	Serving in Colonies.	Serving in France.	Egypt.	Salonika.	Mesopotamia.	East Africa.	Italy.
Tank Corps, H.Q. Signal Company	1	—	—	1	—	—	—	—	—
Tank Brigade Signal Companies	4	—	—	4	—	—	—	—	—
Airline Sections	59	—	—	49	—	8	1	—	1
Light Motor Section	1	—	—	1	—	—	—	—	—
Motor Airline Sections	25	—	—	12	12	—	1	—	—
Cable Sections	89	—	—	65	15	4	3	—	2
Special Cable Section	1	—	—	1	—	—	—	—	—
Indian Cable Section	1	—	—	—	1	—	—	—	—
"L" Signal Battalion	1	—	—	1	—	—	—	—	—
Canadian Army Corps H.Q. Signal Company	1	—	—	1	—	—	—	—	—
Pigeon Service	4	1	—	1	1	1	—	—	—
G.H.Q. Wireless Signal Company	1	—	—	1	—	—	—	—	—
Army Wireless Signal Companies	5	—	—	5	—	—	—	—	—
Cavalry Corps Wireless Signal Squadron	1	—	—	1	—	—	—	—	—
Wireless Signal Establishment	1	—	—	1	—	—	—	—	—
Wireless Signal Companies	2	—	—	1	—	—	—	1	—
G.H.Q. Wireless Observation Groups	4	—	—	1	1	1	1	—	—
Army Wireless Observation Groups	7	—	—	6	—	—	—	—	1
Heavy Artillery Group Signal Sub-sections	95	—	—	88	1	4	—	—	2
Corps Heavy Artillery Signal Sects.	16	—	—	16	—	—	—	—	—
A.F.A. Brigade Signal Sections	41	—	—	41	—	—	—	—	—
Anzac Corps H.A. Signal Sections	2	—	—	2	—	—	—	—	—
R.H.A. Brigade Signal Sub-section	1	—	—	1	—	—	—	—	—
A.H.A. Brigade Signal Sections	3	—	—	1	2	—	—	—	—
Signal Sub-section Royal Naval S.G. Group	1	—	—	1	—	—	—	—	—
Indian Division Signal Companies	2	—	—	—	2	—	—	—	—
Indian Infantry Brigade Signal Cos.	2	—	—	—	2	—	—	—	—
Mounted Brigade Signal Troops	8	—	—	—	5	—	3	—	—
Signal Squadron, Australian Mounted Division	1	—	—	—	1	—	—	—	—
Signal Squadron, 2nd Mounted Division	1	—	—	—	1	—	—	—	—
Signal Section, 1st Imperial Camel Brigade	1	—	—	—	1	—	—	—	—
Yeomanry Mounted Divisional Signal Squadron	1	—	—	—	1	—	—	—	—
Pack Wireless Signal Sections	6	—	—	—	2	4	—	—	—
Wagon Wireless Signal Sections	3	—	—	—	2	1	—	—	—
Northern Wagon Wireless Telegraph Section	1	—	—	—	1	—	—	—	—
Southern Motor Wireless Signal Sect.	1	—	—	—	1	—	—	—	—
Corps Wireless Sections	2	—	—	—	2	—	—	—	—
Wireless Detachment, Hedjaz (with Egyptian Army, for employment)	1	—	—	—	1	—	—	—	—
Western Frontier Force Signal Co.	1	—	—	—	1	—	—	—	—
M. (L. of C.) Signal Company	1	—	—	—	1	—	—	—	—
Palestine (L. of C.) Signal Company	1	—	—	—	1	—	—	—	—
Base Signal Section	1	—	—	—	—	1	—	—	—
Mudros Signal Section	1	—	—	—	—	1	—	—	—
L. of C. Signal Sections	4	—	—	—	—	1	2	—	1
Infantry Brigade Signal Section	1	—	—	—	—	1	—	—	—

GROWTH OF THE ROYAL ENGINEERS—*Continued.*

(c) REGULARS, SPECIAL RESERVE AND TERRITORIAL FORCE (EXCLUSIVE OF THE ROYAL ENGINEERS, TRANSPORTATION BRANCH).

Description of Units.	Number of Units.	Serving at Home.	Serving in Colonies.	Serving in France.	Egypt.	Salonika.	Mesopotamia.	East Africa.	Italy.
Railway Telegraph Detachment	1	—	—	—	—	1	—	—	—
Signal Section R.E. H.Q. Heavy Artillery	1	—	—	—	—	1	—	—	—
Base Wireless Signal Section	1	—	—	—	—	1	—	—	—
Deputy Director of Army Signals	1	—	—	—	—	—	1	—	—
Wireless Signal Squadrons	2	—	—	—	—	—	2	—	—
Imperial Signal Company	1	—	—	—	—	—	—	1	—
Nairobi Signal Company	1	—	—	—	—	—	—	1	—
Nigerian Brigade Signal Section	1	—	—	—	—	—	—	1	—
Telegraph Construction Company	1	—	—	—	—	—	—	—	1
Army Wireless Signal Station (Devizes)	1	1	—	—	—	—	—	—	—
Special Signal Company (Ireland)	1	1	—	—	—	—	—	—	—
"K" Signal Company (Dublin)	1	1	—	—	—	—	—	—	—
Cyclists Brigade Signal Sections	5	5	—	—	—	—	—	—	—
L.A.D.A. Signal Company	1	1	—	—	—	—	—	—	—
Total	1333	168	11	893	116	75	40	9	21

GROWTH OF THE ROYAL ENGINEERS—*Continued.*

(c) REGULARS, SPECIAL RESERVE AND TERRITORIAL FORCE (EXCLUSIVE OF THE ROYAL ENGINEERS, TRANSPORTATION BRANCH)—*continued.*

1st November, 1918.

Strength :—
Officers ... ... } 229,366
Other ranks ... ...

Description of Units.	Number of Units.	Serving at Home.	Serving in Colonies.	Serving in France.	Serving in Egypt.	Salonika.	Mesopotamia.	East Africa.	Italy.
Depôts	20	11	—	6	1	1	1	—	—
Field Companies	224	27	—	161	12	13	6	—	5
Field Company (R.M.R.E.)	1	—	—	1	—	—	—	—	—
Field Company (R.A.R.E.)	1	—	—	1	—	—	—	—	—
Field Squadrons	7	—	—	5	2	—	—	—	—
Army Troops	67	—	—	52	7	7	—	—	1
Army Troops (R.M.R.E.)	2	—	—	2	—	—	—	—	—
Siege Companies (R.M.R.E.)	3	—	—	3	—	—	—	—	—
Siege Companies (R.A.R.E.)	3	—	—	3	—	—	—	—	—
Inspector of Searchlights	1	—	—	1	—	—	—	—	—
Field Searchlight Company	1	—	—	1	—	—	—	—	—
Overseas Branch Ordnance Survey	1	—	—	1	—	—	—	—	—
Field Survey Companies	3	—	—	1	1	1	—	—	—
Field Survey Battalions	5	—	—	5	—	—	—	—	—
Printing Company	1	—	—	1	—	—	—	—	—
Printing Sections	2	—	—	—	1	—	—	1	—
Bridging and Engineer Field Parks	2	—	—	1	—	—	1	—	—
Bridging School	1	—	—	1	—	—	—	—	—
Advanced Park Companies	3	—	—	1	1	1	—	—	—
Base Park Companies	8	—	—	4	2	1	—	1	—
Pontoon Park Companies	13	—	—	11	1	—	—	—	1
Electrical and Mechanical Companies	9	—	—	7	—	—	2	—	—
Water Boring Sections	5	—	—	5	—	—	—	—	—
Waterworks Company	1	—	—	—	1	—	—	—	—
Water Supply Companies	2	—	—	—	2	—	—	—	—
Field Troops	3	—	—	—	2	—	1	—	—
Topographical Section	1	—	—	—	—	—	—	1	—
Reserve Battalions	6	6	—	—	—	—	—	—	—
Reserve Battalion (R.A.R.E.)	1	1	—	—	—	—	—	—	—
Reserve Battalion (R.M.R.E.)	1	1	—	—	—	—	—	—	—
Group Depôt Companies	2	2	—	—	—	—	—	—	—
Army Postal Service (Home Defence)	1	1	—	—	—	—	—	—	—
Foreway Companies	10	—	—	10	—	—	—	—	—
Tunnelling Companies	25	—	—	25	—	—	—	—	—
H.Q. Special Brigade	1	—	—	1	—	—	—	—	—
Battalions Special Brigade	4	—	—	4	—	—	—	—	—
" Z " Special Company	1	—	—	1	—	—	—	—	—
H.Q. Special Companies	1	—	—	1	—	—	—	—	—
Meteorological Sections	4	1	—	1	1	1	—	—	—
Camouflage Park	1	—	—	1	—	—	—	—	—
Special Factory Section	1	—	—	1	—	—	—	—	—
Special Store	1	—	—	1	—	—	—	—	—
Anti-Gas Service	1	—	—	1	—	—	—	—	—
Gas Directorate	1	—	—	1	—	—	—	—	—
Land Drainage Company	1	—	—	1	—	—	—	—	—
Artisan Works Companies	16	—	—	16	—	—	—	—	—
Establishment of Controller of Mines	1	—	—	1	—	—	—	—	—
Army Mine Schools	5	—	—	5	—	—	—	—	—
Forestry Control for Army Areas	1	—	—	1	—	—	—	—	—

GROWTH OF THE ROYAL ENGINEERS—Continued.
(c) REGULARS, SPECIAL RESERVE AND TERRITORIAL FORCE (EXCLUSIVE OF THE ROYAL ENGINEERS, TRANSPORTATION BRANCH).

Description of Units.	Number of Units.	Serving at Home.	Serving in Colonies.	Serving in France.	Serving in Egypt.	Salonika.	Mesopotamia.	East Africa.	Italy.
L. of C. Forestry Group	1	—	—	1	—	—	—	—	—
Directorate of Forestry	1	—	—	1	—	—	—	—	—
L. of C. Forests	1	—	—	1	—	—	—	—	—
Forestry Companies	11	—	—	11	—	—	—	—	—
Anti-Aircraft Searchlight Sections	93	17	—	75	—	—	1	—	—
R.E. Workshops	5	—	—	5	—	—	—	—	—
G.H.Q. 3rd Echelon	4	—	—	1	1	1	1	—	—
H.Q. Divisional Engineers	58	4	—	42	6	4	1	—	1
H.Q. Divisional Engineers (Guards)	1	—	—	1	—	—	—	—	—
Postal Sections	6	1	—	1	1	1	—	1	1
G.H.Q. Kennels (Messenger Dog Service)	1	—	—	1	—	—	—	—	—
Executive Board (British Branch) of the C.I.B.G.	1	—	—	1	—	—	—	—	—
G.S.I. (E) Section G.H.Q.	1	—	—	—	1	—	—	—	—
War Dog School	1	1	—	—	—	—	—	—	—
Fortress Companies	37	27	10	—	—	—	—	—	—
Fortress Works Companies	4	4	—	—	—	—	—	—	—
Works Companies	18	11	1	5	—	—	1	—	—
Telegraph Construction Company	1	—	—	—	—	—	—	—	1
Base Army Anti-Gas School	1	—	—	—	—	1	—	—	—
Divisional Anti-Gas Schools	4	—	—	—	—	4	—	—	—
R.E. Staff, Army Training School	1	—	—	—	—	1	—	—	—
Mining Company	1	—	—	—	—	1	—	—	—
" H " Company (King George's Own Sappers and Miners)	1	—	—	—	—	—	1	—	—
Cinema Company	1	—	—	—	—	—	1	—	—
Emergency Sections	2	2	—	—	—	—	—	—	—
London Electrical Engineers	1	1	—	—	—	—	—	—	—
Tyne Electrical Engineers	1	1	—	—	—	—	—	—	—
Experimental Companies	3	3	—	—	—	—	—	—	—
Cadet Battalion, R.E.	1	1	—	—	—	—	—	—	—
Reserve Survey Company	1	1	—	—	—	—	—	—	—
H.Q. Staff Group, Reserve Field Co.	1	1	—	—	—	—	—	—	—
School of Electric Lighting	1	1	—	—	—	—	—	—	—
Establishment, R.M. College	1	1	—	—	—	—	—	—	—
Establishment, R.M. Academy	1	1	—	—	—	—	—	—	—
R.E. Anti-Gas Establishment	1	1	—	—	—	—	—	—	—
Camouflage School	1	1	—	—	—	—	—	—	—
Base Signal Depôts	6	—	—	2	1	1	1	1	—
Signal Service Training Centre	1	1	—	—	—	—	—	—	—
Divisional Signal Companies	71	5	—	52	7	4	1	—	2
G.H.Q. Signal Companies	5	1	—	1	1	1	—	—	1
Army H.Q. Signal Companies	5	—	—	5	—	—	—	—	—
Army Corps Signal Companies	25	1	—	15	3	2	3	—	1
Indian Infantry Brigade Signal Co.	1	—	—	—	1	—	—	—	—
Army Signal Schools	5	—	—	5	—	—	—	—	—
Corps Signal School	1	—	—	1	—	—	—	—	—
Cavalry Corps Signal School	1	—	—	1	—	—	—	—	—
Cavalry Divisional Signal Squadrons	6	—	—	4	2	—	—	—	—
Signal Construction Companies	5	—	—	5	—	—	—	—	—
Signal Troops	18	2	—	8	5	—	3	—	—
Light Railway Signal Sections	6	—	—	5	1	—	—	—	—
H.Q. Tank Corps Signal Company	1	—	—	1	—	—	—	—	—
Tank Brigade Signal Companies	5	—	—	5	—	—	—	—	—

GROWTH OF THE ROYAL ENGINEERS—Continued.

(c) REGULARS, SPECIAL RESERVE AND TERRITORIAL FORCE (EXCLUSIVE OF THE ROYAL ENGINEERS, TRANSPORTATION BRANCH).

Description of Units.	Number of Units.	Serving at Home.	Serving in Colonies.	Serving in France.	Egypt.	Salonika.	Mesopotamia.	East Africa.	Italy.
Airline Sections	58	—	—	46	—	8	—	—	4
Light Motor Section	1	—	—	1	—	—	—	—	—
Motor Airline Sections	25	—	—	11	12	—	2	—	—
Cable Sections	90	—	—	64	15	4	3	—	4
Special Cable Section	1	—	—	1	—	—	—	—	—
Indian Cable Section	1	—	—	—	1	—	—	—	—
"L" Signal Battalion	1	—	—	1	—	—	—	—	—
Canadian Army Corps, H.Q. Signal Company	1	—	—	1	—	—	—	—	—
Pigeon Services	5	1	—	1	1	1	1	—	—
G.H.Q. Wireless Signal Company	1	—	—	1	—	—	—	—	—
Army Wireless Signal Companies	6	—	—	5	—	—	—	1	—
Cavalry Corps Wireless Signal Squadrons	3	—	—	1	—	—	2	—	—
Wireless Signal Establishment	1	—	—	1	—	—	—	—	—
Wireless Signal Companies	1	—	—	1	—	—	—	—	—
G.H.Q. Wireless Observation Groups	4	—	—	1	1	1	1	—	—
Army Wireless Observation Groups	7	—	—	6	—	—	—	—	1
Heavy Artillery Group Signal Sub-sections	100	—	—	88	3	7	—	—	2
Corps Heavy Artillery Signal Sects.	16	—	—	16	—	—	—	—	—
A.F.A. Brigade Signal Sub-sections	41	—	—	41	—	—	—	—	—
Anzac Corps H.A. Signal Section	1	—	—	1	—	—	—	—	—
R.H.A. Brigade Signal Sub-section	1	—	—	1	—	—	—	—	—
A.H.A. Brigade Signal Sub-sections	2	—	—	2	—	—	—	—	—
Signal Sub-section Royal Naval S.G. Group	1	—	—	1	—	—	—	—	—
Motor Cyclists	2	1	—	1	—	—	—	—	—
G.H.Q. Signal School	1	—	—	—	—	—	—	—	1
(L. of C.) Signal Companies	4	—	—	—	—	1	2	—	1
Wireless Troop—Desert Mounted Corps	1	—	—	—	1	—	—	—	—
Pack Wireless Signal Sections	6	—	—	—	2	4	—	—	—
Wagon Wireless Signal Sections	2	—	—	—	1	1	—	—	—
Northern Wagon Wireless Telegraph Section	1	—	—	—	1	—	—	—	—
Southern Motor Wireless Signal Sect.	1	—	—	—	—	1	—	—	—
Corps Wireless Sections	2	—	—	—	2	—	—	—	—
Wireless Detachment	1	—	—	—	1	—	—	—	—
"M" (L. of C.) Signal Company	1	—	—	—	1	—	—	—	—
Signal Company (L. of C.) South Palestine	1	—	—	—	1	—	—	—	—
Signal Company (L. of C.) Sinai	1	—	—	—	1	—	—	—	—
Base Signal Section	1	—	—	—	—	1	—	—	—
Mudros Signal Section	1	—	—	—	—	1	—	—	—
Infantry Brigade Signal Sections	1	—	—	—	—	1	—	—	—
Railway Telegraph Detachment	1	—	—	—	—	1	—	—	—
Army Signal School	1	—	—	—	—	1	—	—	—
Base Wireless Signal Section	1	—	—	—	—	1	—	—	—
Deputy Director of Army Signals	1	—	—	—	—	—	1	—	—
Army Signal Corps	1	—	—	—	—	—	1	—	—
Wireless Section	1	—	—	—	—	—	1	—	—
School of Signalling	1	—	—	—	—	—	1	—	—
Dunsterforce Signal Section	1	—	—	—	—	—	1	—	—

GROWTH OF THE ROYAL ENGINEERS—*Continued.*

(c) REGULARS, SPECIAL RESERVE AND TERRITORIAL FORCE (EXCLUSIVE OF THE ROYAL ENGINEERS, TRANSPORTATION BRANCH).

Description of Units	Number of Units.	Serving at Home.	Serving in Colonies.	Serving in France.	Serving in				
					Egypt.	Salonika.	Mesopotamia.	East Africa.	Italy.
Imperial Signal Company	1	—	—	—	—	—	—	1	—
Army Wireless Station	1	1	—	—	—	—	—	—	—
Mixed Brigade Signal Sections	6	6	—	—	—	—	—	—	—
Special Signal Companies	2	2	—	—	—	—	—	—	—
Cyclists Divisional Signal Co. (T.)	1	1	—	—	—	—	—	—	—
"K" Signal Company	1	1	—	—	—	—	—	—	—
Cyclist Brigade Signal Sections	11	11	—	—	—	—	—	—	—
L.A.D.A. Signal Company	1	1	—	—	—	—	—	—	—
Special Companies	4	—	—	4	—	—	—	—	—
Total	1338	165	11	899	108	80	41	7	27

www.ingramcontent.com/pod-product-compliance
Lightning Source LLC
Chambersburg PA
CBHW071333190426
43193CB00041B/1767